# Eas
# Arabic Grammar

Jane Wightwick and Mahmoud Gaafar

Illustrations by Mahmoud Gaafar

**McGraw-Hill**

*New York Chicago San Francisco Lisbon London Madrid Mexico City*
*Milan New Delhi San Juan Seoul Singapore Sydney Toronto*

The McGraw-Hill Companies

**Also in this series**
Easy Arabic Script, *Jane Wightwick and Mahmoud Gaafar*



First published in North America 2005 by McGraw-Hill

First published in Great Britain 2005 by Palgrave Macmillan, Houndmills, Basingstoke, Hampshire RG21 6XS

ISBN: 0–07–146210–4

This book is printed on paper suitable for recycling and made from fully managed and sustained forest sources.

Library of Congress Catalog Card Number: On file

Printed and bound in China

# Contents

# Acknowledgements

We would like to thank all those who helped to produce this book. In particular, the input of Ghinwa Mamari of the School of Oriental and African Studies (London University) was invaluable in making the structure of the units more coherent and the trickier grammar points more precise.

Thank you also to Hala Yehia, lecturer in Arabic at the American University in Cairo, for reading the proofs and to Helen Bugler and Isobel Munday at Palgrave Macmillan for their enthusiasm and professionalism.

# Introduction

## What is Arabic 'grammar'?

Arabic 'grammar' will mean different things to different people.

To learners of Arabic as a foreign language it might mean the fundamentals of the language: whether there are genders, whether the noun or the adjective comes first, how the verb changes in the past and future, etc.

To more advanced Arabists and scholars it might mean the higher-level subtleties of Modern Standard or Classical Arabic.

To native speakers, it usually conjures up a subject studied at school, often hazily remembered lessons analysing sentences with a view to being able to spell and pronounce formal Arabic correctly.

What this book means by 'grammar' is a progressive knowledge of the structure of Arabic from the basic building blocks to some, but by no means all, of the more subtle nuances of Modern Standard Arabic.

## Levels of formality

Learners of Arabic generally appreciate the difference between the various spoken Arabic dialects and the universal Modern Standard Arabic. What is not so well understood is that Modern Standard itself can be spoken and written at different levels of sophistication.

Although most Arabs can communicate in a form of standard Arabic and are aware that formal Arabic is pronounced with additional case endings, only scholars, media presenters and public speakers use these endings routinely.

This book includes **Case Notes** sections with additional explanations and activities covering the grammatical case endings used in formal, literary and religious Arabic. These grammatical cases are similar to those found in languages such as German or Russian, but in Arabic are not usually pronounced in less formal contexts. You can use the book without reference to the **Case Notes** if you wish initially to acquire a more general understanding. Alternatively, you can study the **Case Notes** sections if you have an interest in this aspect of Arabic grammar and want to learn about it from the beginning.

## How to use this book

This is a reference and activity book for all beginners and early intermediate students of Arabic, whether studying in a group or by themselves. The book can also be used independently to improve understanding of the basics of grammar or to gain an overview of the structure of the Arabic language.

The book has a built-in progression. Explanations and activities draw only on structures already covered in previous units. Work your way through the units and measure your progress step by step. Alternatively, if you are already studying Arabic you can use the relevant part of the book for extra practice on a particular point of grammar.

The main part of the book is divided into 20 units, each conecentrating on an aspect of Arabic grammar. The units feature:

- clear structural explanations
- more than 100 stimulating activities to practise particular grammar points
- optional **Case Notes** explaining formal case endings (see above)
- end-of-unit **In Summary**, highlighting the most important points of the unit for easy reference.

Answers to all the activities are also included in the final section of the book.

## Arabic script

It is beneficial to acquire familiarity with the Arabic script and the short vowel marks before studying this book. However, the complete alphabet is provided here for reference.

| ***final*** | ***medial*** | ***initial*** | ***isolated*** | ***letter*** |
|---|---|---|---|---|
| ـا | ـا | ا | ا | ألف alif |
| ـب | ـبـ | بـ | ب | باء bā’ |
| ـت | ـتـ | تـ | ت | تاء tā’ |
| ـث | ـثـ | ثـ | ث | ثاء thā’ |
| ـج | ـجـ | جـ | ج | جيم jīm |
| ـح | ـحـ | حـ | ح | حاء ḥā’ |
| ـخ | ـخـ | خـ | خ | خاء khā’ |
| ـد | ـد | د | د | دال dāl |
| ـذ | ـذ | ذ | ذ | ذال dhāl |
| ـر | ـر | ر | ر | راء rā’ |
| ـز | ـز | ز | ز | زاى zāy |
| ـس | ـسـ | سـ | س | سين sīn |
| ـش | ـشـ | شـ | ش | شين shīn |
| ـص | ـصـ | صـ | ص | صاد ṣād |
| ـض | ـضـ | ض | ض | ضاد ḍād |
| ـط | ـطـ | طـ | ط | طاء ṭā’ |
| ـظ | ـظـ | ظـ | ظ | ظاء ẓā’ |

| ***final*** | ***medial*** | ***initial*** | ***isolated*** | ***letter*** |
|---|---|---|---|---|
| ـع | ـعـ | عـ | ع | عين ʿayn |
| ـغ | ـغـ | غـ | غ | غين ghayn |
| ـف | ـفـ | فـ | ف | فاء fā’ |
| ـق | ـقـ | قـ | ق | قاف qāf |
| ـك | ـكـ | كـ | ك | كاف kāf |
| ـل | ـلـ | لـ | ل | لام lām |
| ـم | ـمـ | مـ | م | ميم mīm |
| ـن | ـنـ | نـ | ن | نون nūn |
| ـه | ـهـ | هـ | ه | هاء hā’ |
| ـو | ـو | و | و | واو wāw |
| ـي | ـيـ | يـ | ي | ياء yā’ |

| | |
|---|---|
| فتحة fatḥa | a dash above the letter, pronounced as a short ‘a’ after the letter, e.g. بَـ... ba |
| ضمّة ḍamma | a comma-shape above, pronounced as a short ‘u’ after the letter, e.g. بُـ... bu |
| كسرة kasra | a dash below, pronounced as a short ‘i’ after the letter, e.g. بِـ... bi |
| سكون sukūn | a small circle above showing that *no vowel* follows the letter, e.g. بِنْت bint (girl) |
| شدّة shadda | a small ‘w’ shape above showing that the letter is *doubled*, e.g. بُنّ bunn (coffee beans) |
| مدّة madda | a wavy symbol written over an alif and pronounced ā, e.g. آنسة ānisa (young woman) |

(Note: These symbols are not generally included in modern written Arabic. This book uses them where necessary for clarity.)

part 1

# Fundamentals of Arabic grammar

unit 1

# The Arabic root system

Arabic is a language based on a system of 'roots'. In English, we often refer to the 'root' of a word to mean its origin, for example the root of the English word 'engineer' is the Latin *ingenium*, meaning 'skill'.

The Arabic root, or مصدر maṣdar, refers to the core meaning of a word. This core can usually be identified by three root consonants (non-vowels). For example, the sequence of three consonants س/ف/ر s/f/r (in this order, reading the Arabic script right to left) carries the meaning of 'travel'. A word which includes the sequence of letter س/ف/ر s/f/r is likely to have something to do with travelling. For example:

| | |
|---|---|
| journey | سَفَر safar |
| he travels | يُسافر yusāfir |
| ambassador | سَفير safīr |
| traveller | مُسافِر musāfir |
| embassy | سِفارة sifāra |

All these words are derived from the root س/ف/ر s/f/r. Notice how the root letters always appear in the same order. Any additional consonants or vowels before, after or between the root letters modify the meaning according to different general patterns. The feminine ending ة (tā' marbūṭa) is never part of the root and the most common additional consonants are م m, س s and ت t.

The emphasis on root consonants means that vowels, especially short vowels, are of secondary importance. The pronunciation often varies between Modern Standard Arabic and spoken dialects. For example, يكتب ('he writes') would be pronounced yaktub in Modern Standard, but could be yuktub or yiktib in dialect. The meaning is generally conveyed by the consonants rather than the vowels.

Much of Arabic grammar is concerned with how the root is manipulated to create different related meanings. As you become more familiar with the patterns and structures, you will be more able to identify the roots and to manipulate them yourself.

## *Activity 1*

Can you identify the three root letters in each of the following sets of words? What do you think the general core meaning could be?

| | | |
|---|---|---|
| 1 | book | كِتاب kitāb |
| | office | مكتب maktab |
| | writer/clerk | كاتِب kātib |
| | library | مكتَبة maktaba |
| 2 | lesson | دَرس dars |
| | teacher | مُدَرِّس mudarris |
| | study | دِراسة dirāsa |
| | school | مدَرَسة madrasa |

| | | |
|---|---|---|
| 3 | broken | مكسور maksūr |
| | fragmentation | تكسير taksīr |
| | it was broken | انكسر inkasar |
| | nut cracker | كسّارة kassāra |
| 4 | player | لاعِب lāعib |
| | playing field | ملعَب malعab |
| | toy | لُعبة luعba |
| | games | ألعاب alعāb |

## Words with doubled root letter

Some Arabic words have the same second and third root letters. When this is the case, they are sometimes written together with a shadda doubling sign (ـّ) and sometimes separately, depending on the type of word:

جديد jadīd (new) = *root letters* ج/د/د j/d/d

كلّ kull (all) = *root letters* ك/ل/ل k/l/l

## Words with four root letters

A few Arabic words have four root letters. Sometimes these are four different letters, for example ترجَمة tarjama (translation), where the root letters are ت/ر/ج/م t/r/j/m, but often they are a repeated pair, for example زلزال zalzāl (earthquake), where the root letters are ز/ل/ز/ل z/l/z/l.

## Words of foreign origin

Gernerally loan words such as راديو rādyū (radio) or انترنَت intarnat (internet) fall outside the Arabic root system.

## In summary

- Most Arabic words have a sequence of three root consonants which is connected with a particular core meaning.
- Vowels and consonants are added around the root to create related words and structures.
- The most common additional consonants are م m, س s and ت t.
- Some words have the same second and third root consonants and a few have four root consonants.
- Roots are the building blocks of the Arabic language and are helpful for guessing the meaning of vocabulary.

unit 2

# Gender: masculine and feminine

Arabic nouns (words that name people, objects or ideas) are either *masculine* مُذَكَّر (mudhakkar) or *feminine* مُؤَنَّث (mu'annath).

| | |
|---|---|
| chair *(masculine)* | كُرسي kursī |
| table *(feminine)* | مائِدة mā'ida |

It is not difficult to tell the difference between masculine and feminine words. Feminine words usually fall into one of two categories:

1 Words with the feminine ending ة a (tā' marbūṭa), for example:

| | |
|---|---|
| car | سَيَّارة sayyāra |
| bag | حَقيبة ḥaqība |
| aunt *(maternal)* | خالة khāla |
| nurse *(female)* | مُمَرِّضة mumarriḍa |

2 Words referring to female people but not ending in ة a, for example:

| | |
|---|---|
| girl | بِنت bint |
| mother | أُمّ umm |

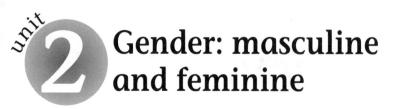

In addition, there are a small number of words which are feminine and don't fit into either of the two feminine categories. Most of these are names of countries, natural features or parts of the body that come in pairs, for example:

| | |
|---|---|
| leg | رِجل rijl |
| sun | شَمس shams |
| desert | صَحراء ṣaḥrā' |
| Egypt | مِصر miṣr |

***Activity 1***

Decide if these words are مُذَكَّر mudhakkar or مُؤَنَّث mu'annath and tick the correct box, as in the example:

| | | | | مُذَكَّر | مُؤَنَّث |
|---|---|---|---|---|---|
| 1 | كتاب kitāb | | book | ☑ | ☐ |
| 2 | أخت ukht | | sister | ☐ | ☐ |
| 3 | بَيت bayt | | house | ☐ | ☐ |
| 4 | قَميص qamīṣ | | shirt | ☐ | ☐ |
| 5 | دَجاجة dajāja | | chicken | ☐ | ☐ |
| 6 | أب ab | | father | ☐ | ☐ |
| 7 | وَلَد walad | | boy | ☐ | ☐ |
| 8 | العِراق al-ع‍irāq | | Iraq | ☐ | ☐ |
| 9 | شارِع shāriع | | street | ☐ | ☐ |
| 10 | صورة ṣūra | | picture | ☐ | ☐ |
| 11 | عَين عayn | | eye | ☐ | ☐ |
| 12 | اِجتِماع ijtimāع | | meeting | ☐ | ☐ |

## Case Notes

Arabic has different levels of formality and complexity. In certain contexts, particularly Quranic or Classical Arabic but also sometimes in more formal Standard Arabic, you will see and hear additional grammatical endings. These endings represent the *case* of the noun (*nominative, accusative* or *genitive*) and whether it is *definite* or *indefinite*. The endings change depending on the function of the noun in a sentence.

Isolated nouns are usually shown with the neutral تَنوين (tanwīn) ending showing they are *indefinite* ('a/an'). تَنوين (tanwīn) literally means 'putting a nūn on' and for this reason is sometimes called *nunation*. It is written as a small symbol above the final letter (ـٌ) and pronounced *un*:

| | |
|---|---|
| a boy | وَلَدٌ walad*un* |
| a girl | بِنتٌ bint*un* |

If a noun ends in ة (tā' marbūṭa), the *t* is pronounced before the تَنوين (tanwīn):

| | |
|---|---|
| a car | سَيَّارَةٌ sayyāra*tun* |
| a nurse | مُمَرِّضَةٌ mumarriḍa*tun* |

تَنوين (tanwīn) is not normally added to foreign loan words such as كمبيوتر kumbyūtir (computer).

**Optional Activity**
Put the تَنوين (tanwīn) on these nouns and say them out loud.

1 قميص
2 دجاجة
3 بيت
4 صورة
5 سيّارة
6 عين

## In summary

- Arabic has two genders: *masculine* and *feminine.*
- Most feminine nouns end in ة (tā marbūṭa) or, if not, they refer to female people, e.g. بنت (bint).
- Other nouns are generally masculine.
- In more formal Standard and Classical Arabic additional grammatical endings may be seen and heard on Arabic nouns.

# unit 3 الـ al- (the)

Arabic has no separate word for 'a' or 'an', as in 'a chair' or 'an apple'. So كِتاب (kitāb) means 'a book', مكتَب (maktab) 'an office', etc.

To make a noun *definite* ('the book', 'the office', etc.), you need to add الـ (al-) meaning 'the'. الـ (al-) is written *joined* to the word it refers to and is the same for both masculine and feminine:

وَلَد walad (a boy) → الولد al-walad (the boy)

بِنت bint (a girl) → البنت al-bint (the girl)

قَميص qamīṣ (a shirt) → القميص al-qamīṣ (the shirt)

حَقيبة ḥaqība (a bag) → الحقيبة al-ḥaqība (the bag)

## Sun letters الحروف الشمسية and moon letters الحروف القمرية

Nouns starting with certain letters of the Arabic alphabet cause the pronunciation of الـ (al-) to change. The 'l' is assimilated and instead the initial letter of the noun is pronounced twice – and written with a shadda (ـّ) if the vowel marks are included:

سَيّارة sayyāra (a car) → السَّيّارة as-sayyāra (the car)

نَهر nahr (a river) → النَّهر an-nahr (the river)

The letters which cause this pronunciation assimilation are called 'sun letters', الحروف الشمسية (al-ḥurūf ash-shamsiyya), as ش (shīn) is itself an assimilating letter. Note that *only* the pronunciation is affected by sun letters. The spelling of الـ (al-) doesn't change. Half the 28 letters of the alphabet are sun letters.

The remainder of the letters are called الحروف القمرية (al-ḥurūf al-qamriyya), as ق (qāf) is not an assimilating letter.

الحروف الشمسية (sun letters):
ت ث د ذ ر ز س ش ص ض ط ظ ل ن

الحروف القمرية (moon letters):
ا ب ج ح خ ع غ ف ق ك م ه و ي

### *Activity 1*

Write these nouns with the article الـ (al-) and then say them out loud, as in the examples.

كرسي **الكرسي** (al-kursī) ____________

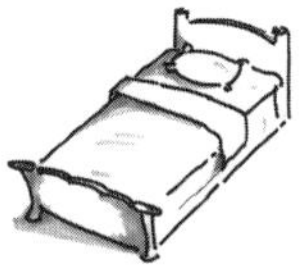
سَرير **السرير** (as-sarīr) ____________

1 
مِفتاح ____________

2 
دَجاجة ____________

3  قَلَم ____________________

4  بَيت ____________________

5  صورة ____________________

6  ممرّضة ____________________

7 

تين ____________________

8  خَيمة ____________________

## Elision

If الـ (al-) comes directly after a vowel, the 'a' of الـ (al-) will drop out, or elide, leaving just the 'l'. Again, this affects only the pronunciation and not the spelling:

al-bayt البيت
(the house)

fi l-bayt في البيت
(in the house)

al-mumarriḍa الممرّضة (the nurse) hiya l-mumarriḍa هِيَ الممرّضة (she [is] the nurse)

## Case Notes

When a noun is made definite (for example, by adding الـ *al-*), the neutral (*nominative*) case ending above the final letter becomes a ḍamma ( ـُ ) pronounced *-u* (*-tu* if the noun ends in ة):

a boy وَلَدٌ walad*un* — the boy الوَلَدُ al-walad*u*

a car سَيَّارَةٌ sayyārat*un* — the car السيّارَةُ as-sayyārat*u*

**Optional Activity**
Put the definite neutral case ending on the answers you gave for Activity 1 and say the words out loud. For example:

1 المفتاحُ al-miftāḥu (the key)

## In summary

- الـ (al-) is the Arabic equivalent of 'the' and is always written joined to the following noun: بيت bayt (house); البيت al-bayt (the house).
- There is no separate word equivalent to 'a/an'.
- Half the letters of the Arabic alphabet assimilate the 'l' of 'al-': التين at-tīn (the figs).
- The 'a' of 'al-' is not pronounced if the previous word ends in a vowel: في البيت fi l-bayt (in the house).

unit 4

# Pronouns (singular) and non-verbal sentences

Pronouns are words such as 'I', 'it' or 'you' which replace names or nouns in a sentence.

Arabic has more pronouns than English since it has different versions for masculine and feminine, singular and plural, and even special *dual* pronouns for two people or things.

## Singular pronouns

Here are the singular pronouns.

| | | |
|---|---|---|
| I | أنا | anā |
| you *(masculine)* | أنتَ | anta |
| you *(feminine)* | أنتِ | anti |
| he, it *(masculine)* | هُوَ | huwa |
| she, it *(feminine)* | هِيَ | hiya |

### *Activity 1*

Cover the pronouns above and then join the Arabic to the English, as in the example.

| | |
|---|---|
| he, it *(masculine)* | أنتِ |
| I | أنا |
| she, it *(feminine)* | هُوَ |
| you *(masculine)* | هِيَ |
| you *(feminine)* | أنتَ |

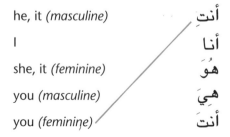

## Non-verbal sentences

You can construct non-verbal sentences in Arabic that do not require the equivalent of ‘am’, ‘are’ or ‘is’. The subject, either a noun or a pronoun, can be followed directly by the rest of the sentence:

| | |
|---|---|
| I [am] Yasmin. | أنا ياسمين.<br>ana yasmīn. |
| Yousef [is a] teacher. | يوسف مُدَرِّس.<br>yūsaf mudarris. |
| My aunt Nadia [is a] nurse. | خالتي نادية مُمَرِّضة.<br>khālatī nādya mumarriḍa. |
| The dog [is] in the garden. | الكَلب في الحَديقة.<br>al-kalb fī l-ḥadīqa. |
| You [are] Ahmed’s father. | أنتَ أبو أحمَد.<br>anta abū aḥmad. |

### *Activity 2*

Fill in the gaps, as in the example.

1 أحمَد مدرّس.

3 ______ أُمّ سارة.

5 هي ______.

## Activity 3

Write out these sentences again using هو or هي, as in the example.

| | |
|---|---|
| هو مدرّس. | 1 أحمَد مُدَرّس. |
| ______ | 2 ياسمين ممرّضة. |
| ______ | 3 الكَلب في الشارِع. |
| ______ | 4 السيّارة في الشارِع. |
| ______ | 5 الوَلَد في الحديقة. |
| ______ | 6 البِنت في السيّارة. |

### Case Notes

Look at these non-verbal sentences with the case endings included:

| | |
|---|---|
| He's a teacher. | هو مُدَرّسٌ. huwa mudarris*un* |
| You're a nurse. | أنتِ مُمَرِّضةٌ. anti mumarriḍa*tun* |
| The girl is in the house. | البِنتُ في البيتِ. al-bint*u* fī l-bayt*i* |

All of the case endings in italics are neutral, or *nominative* – *-un* for indefinite and *-u* for definite – except البيتِ where the ending changes to *-i* after في fī (in). You will learn more about this in Unit 8. For the moment, it is enough to know that the case ending will be nominative unless there is a reason for it *not* to be.

## In summary

- هو huwa means *he* or *it* for masculine nouns;
  هي hiya means *she* or *it* for feminine nouns.
- There are masculine and feminine forms of 'you':
  أنتَ anta *(masculine)* and أنتِ anti *(feminine).*
- There is no direct equivalent of 'is', 'am' or 'are' (verb 'to be' in the present).
- Sentences can be formed without the verb 'to be':
  هو مدرّس. huwa mudarris (He [is a] teacher).

# unit 5 Plurals and plural pronouns

Many aspects of elementary Arabic grammar are straightforward, but plurals require explanation and practice.

The first point to make is that Arabic plurals refer only to three or more people or items. For two people or items, there is a separate dual form, although this is not always used in less formal Arabic. The dual form is covered separately in Unit 13.

## Plural pronouns

In addition to the singular pronouns, there are also five plural pronouns:

| | |
|---|---|
| we | نَحنُ naḥnu |
| you *(masculine plural)* | أنتُم antum |
| you *(feminine plural)* | أنتُنَّ antunna |
| they *(masculine)* | هُم hum |
| they *(feminine)* | هُنَّ hunna |

Although there are separate masculine and feminine plural forms of 'you' and 'they', the masculine is the most common. If a group of people is mixed male and female, the masculine form is used. The group must be entirely female for the feminine plural to be used. (Spoken dialects sometimes ignore even this difference and use the masculine form throughout.)

## Plural nouns: introduction

Arabic nouns can be made plural in one of two ways:

- By adding a *suffix* (ending) to the singular noun, similar to the way English adds '-s' to 'tree' to produce 'trees' or '-es' to 'box' to produce 'boxes'. This is called the *sound plural* (al-jamع as-sālim الجمع السالم).
- By changing the internal vowels of the singular word, similar to the way English turns 'mouse' into 'mice' or 'man' into 'men'. This is called the *broken plural* (jamع at-taksīr جمع التكسير)

However, whereas 'mouse/mice' is the exception in English, the broken plural is common in Arabic and accounts for the majority of plurals, particularly of basic words.

The simpler sound plural will be covered in this unit and the broken plural in Unit 11.

## Sound plurals

There are two sound plurals, formed by adding external suffixes:

- *sound masculine plural*
- *sound feminine plural*

### *Sound masculine plural*

The sound masculine plural is formed by adding ون -ūn or ين -īn to the singular noun:

مدرّس mudarris → مدرّسون mudarrisūn / مدرّسين mudarrisīn
(male teacher) (teachers)

The alternative ين -īn ending is used in particular structures which will be explained later in this book.

The sound masculine plural (SMP) is used almost exclusively with words describing groups of males or mixed males and females, for example when referring to jobs and nationalities:

محاسب muḥāsib → محاسبون muḥāsibūn / محاسبين muḥāsibīn
(accountant) (accountants)

عراقيّ عirāqīy → عراقيّون عirāqīyūn / عراقيّين عirāqīyīn
(Iraqi) (Iraqis)

Note that not all words describing male people can be made plural using the SMP. Some use a broken plural (see Unit 11).

## *Activity 1*

Complete these sentences using the plural of the words in the box, as in the example. (All of the words can be made plural using the sound masculine -ūn ending.)

| | |
|---|---|
| engineer | مُهندِس muhandis |
| carpenter | نَجّار najjār |
| baker | خَبّاز khabbāz |
| Egyptian | مصريّ muṣrīy |
| French | فَرَنسيّ faransīy |

هُم مدرّسون. ____

____ 1

2

3

4

5

## *Sound feminine plural*

The sound feminine plural (SFP) is formed by adding ات -āt to the singular. If the singular word ends with the feminine -a (ـة), this should be removed before the SFP is added:

جُنَيه junayh (pound) → جنيهات junayhāt (pounds)

ممرّضة mumarriḍa (nurse) → ممرّضات mumarriḍāt (nurses)

سَيّارة sayyāra (car) → سَيّارات sayyārāt (cars)

Unlike the name 'sound feminine plural' suggests, this ending is *not* used exclusively to make feminine nouns plural. It is a common plural and is used with both feminine and masculine nouns, although not generally with nouns referring to male people. There are two main groups of nouns with which the SFP is used.

### SFP with all-female groups of people

The SFP is used for groups of three of more females:

مدرّسة mudarrisa → مدرّسات mudarrisāt
(female teacher) (female teachers)

عِراقيّة ɛirāqīyya → عراقيّات ɛirāqīyāt
(female Iraqi) (female Iraqis)

## *Activity 2*

Make these sentences feminine using the SFP, as in the example.

هُم مدرّسون. ← **هُنّ مدرّسات.**

1 هم مُحاسبون. ______

2 نَحنُ عراقيّون. ______

3 هم فَرَنسيّون. ______

4 أنتُم مصريّون؟ ______

5 لا، نَحنُ كُويتيّون. ______

6 هم مُهندِسون. ______

**SFP with masculine and feminine non-human nouns**
The SFP is commonly used with a variety of masculine and feminine words referring to objects or ideas.

زُجاجة zujāja (bottle) → زُجاجات zujājāt (bottles)

اجتِماع ijtimāع (meeting) → اجتِماعات ijtimāعāt (meetings)

حَيَوان ḥayawān (animal) → حَيَوانات ḥayawānāt (animals)

لُغة lugha (language) → لُغات lughāt (languages)

سيّارة sayyāra (car) → سيّارات sayyarāt (cars)

ثلاجة thallāja (fridge) → ثلاجات thallājāt (fridges)

Unfortunately there are no hard-and-fast rules for knowing which nouns use the SFP, although you will get a better feel as your knowledge of the structure of Arabic increases. You need to learn each word individually with its plural.

In informal contexts you may also hear and see foreign loan words with the SFP ات -āt ending:

| | |
|---|---|
| تليفون tilīfūn → (telephone) | تليفونات tilīfūnāt (telephones) |
| كُمبيوتِر kumbyūtir → (computer) | كُمبيوتِرات kumbyūtirāt (computers) |

## Non-human plurals

Plural pronouns such as هُم hum and هُن hunna are only used when referring to humans, e.g. هُم مدرّسون hum mudarrisūn (they're teachers). With non-human plurals, Arabic uses the *feminine singular* pronoun, e.g. أين الزُجاجات؟ هِيَ في الثلاجة. ayna az-zujājāt? *hiya* fī th-thalāja (Where are the bottles? *They're* in the fridge).

This feature extends to *all* grammatical structures, such as verbs and adjectives (which will be covered in later units). The feminine singular is used with all non-human plurals whether the nouns are originally masculine or feminine in the singular.

## *Activity 3*

Make sentences using هُوَ huwa, هِيَ hiya, هُم hum or هُنَّ hunna, as in the example.

1 هِيَ مُحاسبة.

2 ______________.

3 ______________.

4 ______________.

5 أينَ القلم؟

______________.

6 أينَ القطّة؟

______________.

7 أينَ السيّارات؟

______________.

## Case Notes

Plural nouns also have case endings. The neutral nominative ending for the sound feminine plural is *-un/-u* as it is for singular nouns:

| | | |
|---|---|---|
| nurses | ممرّضاتٌ | mumarriḍāt*un* |
| the nurses | الممرّضاتُ | al-mumarriḍāt*u* |

However, the nominative ending for the sound masculine plural is *-ūn* for both indefinite and definite:

| | | |
|---|---|---|
| teachers | مدرّسون | mudarris*ūn* |
| the teachers | المدرّسون | al-mudarris*ūn* |

The sound masculine plural is one of the few instances of the case ending being written as part of the main script and universally pronounced.

**Optional Activity**
Make these words plural and pronounce them with the indefinite case ending:

1 زُجاجة (bottle)
2 خبّاز (baker)
3 حَيَوان (animal)
4 لُغة (language)
5 مُهَندِس (male engineer)
6 سيّارة (car)
7 مُدَرِّسة (female teacher)
8 اجتِماع (meeting)

## In summary

- There are two types of plural in Arabic, external 'sound' plurals and internal 'broken' plurals. There are no precise rules governing which plural is used for a particular noun.
- The sound masculine plural (SMP) is formed by adding ون/ين -ūn/-īn to the singular and is used with nouns referring to groups of people.
- The sound feminine plural (SFP) is formed by adding ات -āt to the singular (after any ة tā marbūṭa has been removed). The SFP is used with groups of females and to make certain other masculine and feminine nouns plural.
- Arabic grammar treats any non-human plural as *feminine singular*. So you must use the feminine singular pronoun هي hiya with the plural of objects:

  أين السيّارات؟ هي في الشارع.

  (Where are the cars? **They** are in the street.)

unit 6

# Demonstratives

Demonstratives are the equivalents of the English 'this' or 'that', as in 'this house', 'that boy'.

Arabic demonstratives change according to whether they are describing a feminine or a masculine word:

| | |
|---|---|
| this *(masculine)* | هذا hādha |
| this *(feminine)* | هذه hādhihi |
| that *(masculine)* | ذلك dhālika |
| that *(feminine)* | تلك tilka |

The demonstratives go in front of the noun with the article الـ.. (al):

| | |
|---|---|
| this boy | هذا الولد hādha l-walad |
| this girl | هذه البنت hādhihi l-bint |
| that house | ذلك البيت dhālika l-bayt |
| that city | تلك المدينة tilka l-madīna |

Notice how the a of الـ.. (al) elides as the demonstratives all end in a vowel (see Unit 3).

## *Activity 1*

Fill in the gaps with the correct Arabic demonstrative to match the English, as in the example:

| | | | |
|---|---|---|---|
| this man | الرَجُل | هذا | 1 |
| this bag | الحَقيبة | ............ | 2 |
| that newspaper | الجَريدة | ............ | 3 |
| that teacher | المُدَرِّس | ............ | 4 |
| that nurse | المُمَرِّضة | ............ | 5 |
| this pen | القَلَم | ............ | 6 |
| this river | النَهر | ............ | 7 |
| that shirt | القَميص | ............ | 8 |

The demonstratives can also be used with an indefinite noun without الـ (al) to form a sentence:

| | | |
|---|---|---|
| This [is a] boy. | هذا ولد. | hādha walad. |
| That [is a] city. | تلك مدينة. | tilka madīna. |

You need to be careful. As you already know, Arabic has no separate word for 'a/an' or direct equivalent of 'is/are'. This means that only the presence of الـ (al) indicates the difference between:

| | | |
|---|---|---|
| a) this book | هذا الكِتاب | hādha l-kitāb |
| b) This [is a] book. | هذا كِتاب. | hādha kitāb. |

If you want to say ‘This is *the* book’, etc. you need to add هو huwa (masculine) or هي hiya (feminine) after the demonstrative:

| | |
|---|---|
| This [is] the bag. | هذه هي الحقيبة.<br>hādhihi hiya l-ḥaqība. |
| That [is] the man. | ذلك هو الرجل.<br>dhālika huwa r-rajul. |

## *Activity 2*

Write sentences to match the pictures, as in the example. Pay special attention as to whether the object is near (“this”) or far away (“that”).

1

هذه بنت.

2

3

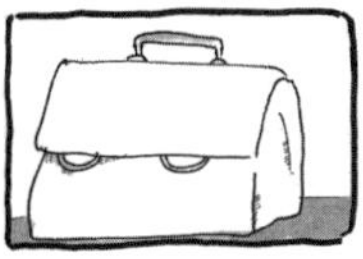
4

5

6

7

8

## Case Notes

If the case endings are added to demonstrative sentences, the ending will vary according to whether the noun is definite (with 'al') or indefinite:

| | |
|---|---|
| This is a boy. | هذا ولدٌ. hādha walad*un*. |
| This man is an engineer. | هذا الرجلُ مهندسٌ.<br>hādha r-rajul*u* muhandis*un*. |
| That is a river. | ذلك نهرٌ. dhālika nahr*un*. |

Remember that if a noun ends in ة (tā marbūṭa), the tā becomes "untied" before a case ending and is pronounced as a 't' (see Unit 2):

| | |
|---|---|
| That girl is a nurse. | تلك البنتُ ممرّضةٌ.<br>tilka l-bint*u* mumarriḍa*tun*. |
| This city is large. | هذه المدينةُ كبيرةٌ.<br>hādhihi l-madīna*tu* kabīra*tun*. |

**Optional Activity**

Put the case endings on these sentences:

1 هذا قلم.

2 ذلك ولد.

3 هذا الرجل خبّاز.

4 هذه مدرّسة.

5 تلك الحقيبة كبيرة.

## Demonstratives with the plural

Remember that Arabic distinguishes between human and non-human plurals. Non-human plurals are grammatically *feminine singular* (see Unit 5).

So, for non-humans, the demonstratives will be the same as the feminine singular, i.e. هذه hādhihi and تلك tilka:

| | |
|---|---|
| these meetings | هذه الاجتماعات<br>hādhihi l-ijtimāɛāt |
| These are bottles. | هذه زجاجات.<br>hādhihi zujājāt. |
| Those cars are comfortable. | تلك السيارات مريحة.<br>tilka s-sayyārāt murīḥa. |

When talking about people, you will see the following plural demonstratives:

| | |
|---|---|
| these *(human plural)* | هؤلاء hā'ulā'i |
| those *(human plural)* | أولئك ulā'ika |
| these nurses | هؤلاء الممرّضات<br>hā'ulā'i l-mumarriḍāt |
| Those are the teachers. | أولئك هم المدرّسون.<br>ulā'ika hum al-mudarrisūn. |

The plural demonstratives are difficult to spell and pronounce. As a beginner, the most important aspect is learning to recognise them.

## *Activity 3*

Look at the pictures and decide if the sentences are true or false, as in the example:

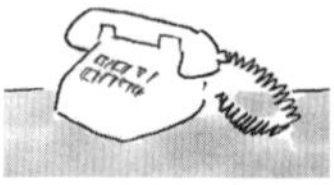
☒ 1 هذا قلم.

☐ 2 هذه جريدة.

☐ 3 هذا قميص.

☐ 4 ذلك الرجل مدرّس.

☐ 5 هذه سيّارات.

☐ 6 هؤلاء مدرّسون.

☐ 7 ذلك بيت.

☐ 8 أولئك ممرّضات.

## In summary

- Arabic demonstratives change according to whether the noun is masculine or feminine, singular, plural or dual.

- The most common demonstratives are:
  *masculine singular:* هذا hādha (this); ذلك dhālika (that)
  *feminine singular* <u>and</u> *non-human plurals*:
  هذه hādhihi (this); تلك tilka (that)

- Plural demonstratives are only used with nouns referring to *humans*:
  هؤلاء hā'ulā'i (this); أولئك ulā'ika (that)

- The meaning changes depending on whether the noun has the article ال al-:

  هذا الولد hādha l-walad (this boy)
  هذا ولد. hādha walad. (This is a boy.)

unit 7

# Adjectives and descriptive sentences

Descriptive words such as 'beautiful', 'new' or 'heavy' are known in English as *adjectives*.

A feature of Arabic adjectives is that many display common patterns. One of the most basic of these patterns is a fatha (a) after the first consonant and a long ـيـ (ī) between the second and third consonants:

| | | |
|---|---|---|
| beautiful | jamīl | جميل |
| ugly | qabīḥ | قبيح |
| new | jadīd | جديد |
| old | qadīm | قديم |
| heavy | thaqīl | ثقيل |
| light | khafīf | خفيف |
| big/large | kabīr | كبير |
| small | ṣaghīr | صغير |
| tall/long | ṭawīl | طويل |
| short | qaṣīr | قصير |

Adjectives also often begin with مَـ ma- or مُـ mu- (the equivalent of the English past participle as in 'broken' or 'burnt' – see Unit 19):

| | | |
|---|---|---|
| broken | maksūr | مكسور |
| happy | masrūr | مَسرور |
| famous | mash-hūr | مَشهور |
| married | mutazawwij | مُتَزَوِّج |
| suitable | munāsib | مُناسِب |

## Position and agreement of adjectives

In English, adjectives are placed in front of the noun they describe: 'beautiful river', 'new teacher'. In Arabic, descriptive words are placed *after* the noun and must 'agree' with it. In other words, if the noun is feminine, the adjective must also be made feminine, usually by adding ة:

| | | |
|---|---|---|
| (a) beautiful river | nahr jamīl | نهر جميل |
| (a) beautiful girl | bint jamīla | بنت جميلة |
| (a) new teacher | mudarris jadīd | مدرّس جديد |
| (a) new car | sayyāra jadīda | سيّارة جديدة |

These descriptive words can be used to describe a noun directly, as in the above examples (known in Arabic as الصفة aṣ-ṣifa), or as the *predicate* of a sentence (known in Arabic as الخبر al-khabar, "the news"). الخبر al-khabar is the part of the sentence that carries the information:

| | | |
|---|---|---|
| The river [is] beautiful. | an-nahr jamīl. | النهر جميل. |
| The car [is] new. | as-sayyāra jadīda. | السيّارة جديدة. |

## *Activity 1*

Look at the list of adjectives on pages 34–5 and then fill in the gaps to match the pictures, as in the example. (There may be more than one possible answer.)

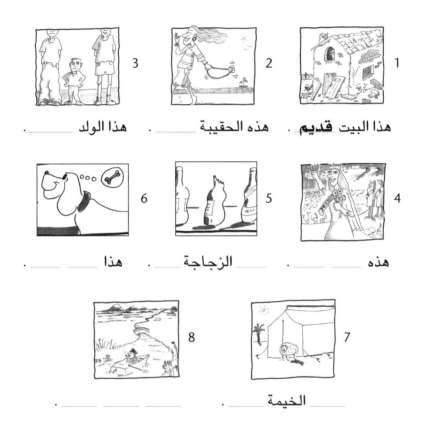

1

هذا البيت **قديم** .

2

هذه الحقيبة ______ .

3

هذا الولد ______ .

4

هذه ______ ______ .

5

______ الزجاجة ______ .

6

هذا ______ ______ .

7

______ الخيمة ______ .

8

______ ______ ______ .

## Adjectives with definite nouns

If an adjective is describing a definite noun with الـ al ('the') as in البيت al-bayt (the house), then the adjective must also have الـ al:

| | | |
|---|---|---|
| the new teacher | al-mudarris al-jadīd | المدرّس الجديد |
| the beautiful picture | aṣ-ṣūra al-jamīla | الصورة الجميلة |

When a noun has a possessive ending, as in بيتي baytī (my house), the noun is definite since we know which house is referred to. In this case, the adjective will also need to begin with الـ al:

بيتي الجديد في شارع قريب من المدرسة الكبيرة.
baytī al-jadīd fī shāriع qarīb min al-madrasa al-kabīra.
My new house is in a street near to the large school.

More details on possessive endings can be found in Unit 10.

If there is more than one adjective, they can all be added after the noun, usually separated by وَ wa- ('and'):

| | |
|---|---|
| a large new school | مدرسة كبيرة وجديدة<br>madrasa kabīra wa-jadīda |
| the beautiful old chair | الكرسي الجميل والقديم<br>al-kursī al-jamīl wal-qadīm |

You need to be very careful about where you place الـ al- and هذا/هذه hādhā/hādhihi as the structure, and so also the meaning, will be affected:

| | |
|---|---|
| a beautiful river | نهر جميل<br>nahr jamīl |
| the beautiful river | النهر الجميل<br>an-nahr al-jamīl |
| The river is beautiful. | النهر جميل.<br>an-nahr jamīl. |
| This is a beautiful river. | هذا نهر جميل.<br>hādhā nahr jamīl. |
| This river is beautiful. | هذا النهر جميل.<br>hādhā n-nahr jamīl. |

### Activity 2

Match the Arabic with the English:

| | |
|---|---|
| a) a large car | ١ هذا الرجل متزوّج. |
| b) the famous river | ٢ البنت الصغيرة مسرورة. |
| c) The bag is light. | ٣ النهر المشهور |
| d) This newspaper is old. | ٤ البيت الجديد قبيح. |
| e) This man is married. | ٥ هذه الجريدة قديمة. |
| f) The small girl is happy. | ٦ سيّارة كبيرة. |
| g) The new house is ugly. | ٧ الحقيبة خفيفة. |

## Adjectives with plurals

Plural adjectives are used only with people. Remember that non-human plurals are always treated as feminine singular (see Unit 5) and so will be followed by a feminine singular adjective:

| | | |
|---|---|---|
| a long meeting | ijtimāع ṭawīl | اجتماع طويل |
| long meetings | ijtimāعāt ṭawīla | اجتماعات طويلة |
| the broken bottle | az-zujāja al-maksūra | الزجاجة المكسورة |
| the broken bottles | az-zujājāt al-maksūra | الزجاجات المكسورة |

Plural adjectives for describing people can often be formed using the sound masculine and sound feminine plurals (see Unit 5), but some of the basic adjectives have broken plurals which need to be individually learnt (see Unit 11). For now it is enough to understand the basic principle and recognise the difference:

| | |
|---|---|
| Lebanese boys | أولاد لُبنانيون<br>awlād lunbānīyūn |
| new engineers | مهندسون جُدُد<br>muhandisūn judud |
| the suitable nurses | الممرضات المناسبات<br>al-mumarriḍāt al-munāsibāt |

## *Activity 3*

Read this description of Nadia (نادية) from Beirut (بيروت) in Lebanon. Use the correct form of the adjective in brackets to complete the paragraph, as in the example.

نادية من بيروت.
بيروت مدينة **كبيرة** (كبير)
و ________ (جميل).
نادية مُدرّسة في مَدرسة
________ (صغير). بيت نادية
________ (قديم) و ________
(قريب) من البَنك ________
(لُبناني) والمَصنَع ________
(جديد). نادية ________ (متزوّج) وهي ________ (مسرور)
في عَمَلها بالمدرسة.

*مصنَع maṣnā = factory

## Colours

Adjectives describing the basic colours have a somewhat different pattern to other adjectives. They begin with a (أ) and have another 'a' between the second and third consonants:

أحمَر aḥmar (red). They have their own special feminine form (also used with non-human plurals).

| *colour* | *masculine* | *feminine + plural (non-human)* |
| --- | --- | --- |
| red | أحمَر aḥmar | حَمراء ḥamrā' |
| blue | أزرَق azraq | زَرقاء zarqā' |
| green | أخضَر akhḍar | خَضراء khaḍrā' |
| yellow | أصفَر aṣfar | صَفراء ṣafrā' |
| black | أسوَد aswad | سوداء sawdā' |
| white | أبيَض abyaḍ | بيضاء bayḍā' |

## *Activity 4*

Make sentences as in the example. You can colour the objects first if you prefer. (Note: pens = أقلام aqlām)

1 *green*  هذا الكتاب أخضر.

2 *red*  ______________

3 *yellow*  ______________

4 *blue*  ______________

5 *black*  ______________

6 *green*  ______________

7 *yellow + blue*  ______________

8 *black + white*  ______________

## Case Notes

Case endings for adjectives match that of the noun described:

a beautiful river نهرٌ جميلٌ nahr*un* jamīl*un*

the old newspaper الجريدةُ القديمةُ al-jarīda*tu* l-qadīma*tu*

In the following sentences the descriptive word is الخبر al-khabar (the predicate), and so it is indefinite:

This river is beautiful. هذا النهرُ جميلٌ hādhā n-nahr*u* jamīl*un*

The newspaper is old. الجريدةُ قديمةٌ al-jarīda*tu* qadīma*tun*

Colours are an exception. The nominative case ending is *-u* for both indefinite <u>and</u> definite:

a red pen قلمٌ أحمرُ qalam*un* aḥmar*u*

this yellow book هذا الكتابُ الأصفرُ hādhā l-kitāb*u* l-aṣfar*u*

**Optional Activity**
Put the case endings on the sentences in *Activity 2*, for example:

(hādhā r-rajul*u* mutazawwij*un*). ١ هذا الرجلُ متزوّجٌ.

## In summary

- Arabic adjectives are placed after the noun they describe and agree with the noun, usually adding *-a* (ة) for a feminine noun and non-human plurals.
- The definite article الـ al- should be added to the adjective if the noun described is definite.
- The plurals of adjectives are used only when describing people.
- Adjectives describing basic colours have a distinctive pattern and their own feminine forms, e.g. aḥmar/ḥamrā' أحمر/حمراء (red).

unit 8

# Describing position

Words such as 'under', 'in' and 'on' are used to describe position. Common words used to describe position in Arabic include:

| | |
|---|---|
| in | في fī |
| on | على ealā |
| under | تَحت taḥta |
| above | فَوق fawqa |
| in front of | أمامَ amāma |
| behind | وَراءَ warā'a |
| next to | بِجانِب bijānib |
| between | بَينَ bayna |
| from | مِن min |
| to | إلى ilā |

Arabic positional sentences work in a similar way to English ones. Note that since many of the positional words end with a short or long vowel, the a of the following al- elides.

| | |
|---|---|
| The newspaper [is] on the chair. | الجريدة على الكُرسي.<br>al-jarīda ɛalā l-kursī. |
| There [is] a dog under the table. | هناك كلب تَحتَ المائدة.<br>hunāka kalb taḥta l-mā'ida. |
| Al-Manama [is] in Bahrain. | المنامة في البحرين.<br>al-manāma fī l-baḥrayn. |

على ɛalā (on) and إلى ilā (to) can also be combined with يَمين yamīn (right) and يَسار yasār (left):

| | |
|---|---|
| The school is on the left. | المَدرسة على اليسار.<br>al-madrasa ɛalā l-yasār. |
| We went to the right. | ذَهَبْنا إلى اليمين.<br>dhahabnā ilā l-yamīn. |

***Activity 1***

Draw the objects in the correct position to match the sentence, as in the example:

١ هناك زجاجة تحت الكرسي.

٢ هناك كلب على المائدة.

٣ القلم في الحقيبة.

٤ هناك سيّارات أمام البيت.

٥ السرير بجانب الباب
على اليمين.

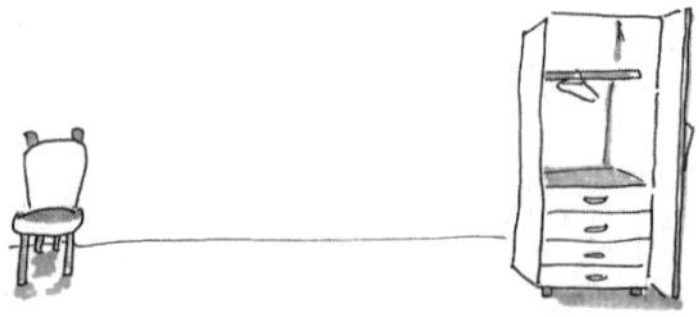

٦ الشبّاك بين الخزانة
والكرسي.

## *Activity 2*

Rearrange the Arabic into sentences to match the English meaning, as in the example.

1 بجانب / البنك / المدرسة / الجديد

**البنك الجديد بجانب المدرسة.**

The new bank is next to the school.

2 في / مهندس / السيّارات / فيصل / مصنع

____________________

Faisal is an engineer in the car factory.

3 لبنان/نادية/من/في/بيروت

---

Nadia is from Beirut in Lebanon.

4 صغيرة/فوق/هناك/الشبّاك/صورة

---

There's a small picture above the window.

5 إلى/قديمة/ذهبنا/مدينة

---

We went to an old town.

6 حقيبة/على/هناك/الكرسي/ثقيلة

---

There's a heavy bag on the table.

## *Activity 3*

Look at the scene below:

Now choose the correct word from the box to complete the description of the scene on page 45, as in the example.

| | | | | | |
|---|---|---|---|---|---|
| كبيرة | فوق | على | الأسود | هناك | ~~شارع~~ |
| البيت | بنت | قديم | السيّارة | وراء | درّاجة |

هذا **شارع** كبير. في وَسَط الشارع _______ مَتحَف (museum).

هناك شجر طويل _______ المتحف وولد على _______ أمام

المتحف. هناك مدرسة _______ بجانب المتحف.

_______ يمين المتحف هناك بيت _______ وجميل.

الرجل مَعَ (with) الكلب _______ أمام _______.

وهناك طائِرة (airplane) _______ البيت.

في الشارع هناك سيّارات وفي _______ البيضاء هناك

إمرَأة (woman) و_______ .

## Case Notes

The grammatical case endings of nouns and adjectives change after positional words. The nominative endings *(t)un* (ـٌ) or *(t)u* (ـُ) on the noun or adjective become *(t)in* (ـٍ) or *(t)i* (ـِ).

These case endings are known as مجرور majrūr in Arabic and as *genitive* in English. The genitive is used after prepositions and positional words (and when describing possession which will be covered in Unit 10).

| | | |
|---|---|---|
| under a table | taḥt mā'ida*tin* | تحت مائدةٍ |
| in the old house | fī l-bayt*i* l-qadīm*i* | في البيتِ القديمِ |
| behind the cars | warā'a s-sayyārāt*i* | وراء السيّاراتِ |

Look at these example sentences with the case endings added:

| | |
|---|---|
| The newspaper [is] on the table. | الجريدةُ على المائدةِ. al-jarīda*tu* ؏alā l-mā'ida*ti*. |
| There [is] a dog in the house. | هناك كلبٌ في البيتِ. hunāka kalb*un* fī l-bayt*i*. |
| He is a teacher in a new school. | هو مدرّسٌ في مدرسةٍ جديدةٍ. huwa mudarris*un* fī madrasa*tin* jadīda*tin*. |

Remember that case endings are not normally added to words of foreign origin such as راديو (rādyū) or تليفون (tilīfūn).

**Optional Activity**
Read these sentences with the case endings and say what they mean in English.

١ البنت في المدرسة.

٢ هناك قلم على المائدة.

٣ الولد بين الشبّاك والباب.

٤ ذَهَبنا إلى المدينة.

٥ هناك نهر جميل في المدينة.

٦ هناك مصنع جديد بجانب النهر.

## In summary

- Positional words such as في fī (in) and على ؏alā (on) describe position.
- Arabic positional sentences are formed in a similar way to English ones.

# unit 9 Forming questions

Questions are relatively simple to form in Arabic. There is no special question form, such as the English 'do/does?' or 'did?', and the order of words is generally not affected.

## Yes/no questions

Questions requiring only the answer نَعم naɛm (yes) or لا lā (no) can be made in one of two ways:

1 Adding a question mark at the end of a statement (or orally adding a question tone). This is most common in less formal Arabic:

| | |
|---|---|
| Khartoum is in Sudan? | الخرطوم في السودان؟<br>al-kharṭūm fī s-sūdān? |
| This car is new? | هذه السيّارة جديدة؟<br>hādhihi s-sayyāra jadīda? |

2 Adding the question marker هَل hal (or less commonly أ a) in front of a statement:

| | |
|---|---|
| Is the cat in the house? | هَل القطّة في البيت؟<br>hal al-qiṭṭa fī l-bayt? |
| Is there a bank near the office? | هَل هناك بنك قريب من المكتب؟<br>hal hunāka bank qarīb min al-maktab? |
| Are you Mahmoud? | أأنتَ محمود؟<br>a-anta maḥmūd? |

Note that أ a is written as part of the following word, as are all Arabic words that consist of only one letter.

## *Activity 1*

Answer the questions as in the example.

1  هل القطّة تحت الكرسي؟ **نعم، هي تحت الكرسي.**

2  هم مُحاسبون؟ ______________________

3  هل السيّارة بيضاء؟ ______________________

4  أهذا كتاب؟ ______________________

5 

هل البنك وراء الشجر؟ ______________________

6  الكلب أبيض؟ ______________________

## Question words

Other questions begin with a specific question word, such as أينَ؟ ayna? (where?) or مَن man? (who?). In this case, the question markers هَل hal or أ a are not used:

| | |
|---|---|
| Where's Damascus?<br>It's in Syria. | أينَ دِمَشق؟ هي في سوريا.<br>ayna dimashq? hiya fī sūriyā. |
| Who's this?<br>This is my brother. | مَن هذا؟ هذا أخي.<br>man hādhā? hādhā akhī. |

Some of the more commonly used question words include:

| | |
|---|---|
| where? | أين؟ ayna |
| who? | مَن؟ man |
| what? | ما/ ماذا؟ mā/mādhā |
| why? | لِماذا؟ limādhā |
| when? | مَتى؟ matā |
| how? | كَيفَ؟ kayfa |
| how many? | كم؟ kam |
| how much? (price) | بِكم؟ bikam |
| which? | أيّ؟ ayy |

Note that there are two question words meaning 'what'. ما؟ mā is used with a following noun and ماذا؟ mādhā mainly with a verb:

| | |
|---|---|
| What's your address? | ما عُنوانك؟ mā ع unwānak? |
| What are you doing? | ماذا تَفعَل؟ mādhā tafعal? |

كَم؟ kam (how many?) is followed by a *singular* noun. In addition the noun has a special ending ـً -(t)an known as tanwīn al-fatḥ. This ending carries the meaning of 'as to' or 'regarding' and is written on an extra alif (اً) if the noun does not end in ta' marbūṭa. This is one of the few examples of the system of Arabic case endings affecting the basic spelling and pronunciation. The Case Notes in this unit will give you further details, or you can just remember when to use tanwīn al-fatḥ on a case-by-case basis:

| | | |
|---|---|---|
| How many boys? | كَم ولداً؟ | kam walad*an*? |
| How many schools? | كَم مَدرسةً؟ | kam madrasa*tan*? |

(In less formal spoken Arabic tanwīn al-fatḥ is not usually pronounced.)

## *Activity 2*

Fill in the appropriate question word, as in the example.

١ **أينَ** البنت؟ هي في المدرسة.

٢ ______ اسمك؟ اسمي أحمد.

٣ ______ هذا؟ هذا أخي.

٤ ______ ولداً في المدرسة؟

٥ ______ التين *(figs)*؟ التين بخمسة جنيهات.

٦ ______ حالك؟ أنا بِخَير.

٧ ______ ذهبتَ *(did you go)* إلى مصر؟ في مايو.

٨ ______ ذهبتَ إلى مصر؟ لأنّ *(because)* أمّي مِصريّة.

## *Activity 3*

Now make questions to suit the answers, as in the example.

١ أنا من السودان. **أنت من أين؟**

٢ هو من أمريكا. ______

٣ هناك ١٠ زجاجات على المائدة. ______

٤ السيّارة في الشارِع. ______________

٥ الحَفلة الساعة الثالثة. ______________
(The party is at 3 o'clock.)

٦ نعم. هناك بنك في المدينة. ______________

٧ كَتَبَ أحمد الرسالة. ______________

## Case Notes

The third, and final, case in Arabic is known as النصب an-naṣb, or the *accusative.* The indefinite accusative is vowelled with two fatḥas (ـً) and pronounced *(t)an.* كَم؟ kam (how many?) is followed by a singular noun in the indefinite accusative.

An unusual feature of the accusative case is that the indefinite ending is written on an extra alif ( اً alif tanwīn). The exception is if the noun already ends in the feminine ة tā marbūṭa:

| | |
|---|---|
| how many men? | كم رجلاً؟ kam rajul*an* |
| how many cars? | كم سيّارةً؟ kam sayyārat*an* |

**Optional Activity**
Ask how many there are of the following items, as in the example. Remember to use a singular noun with the accusative case ending:

١  كم بنتاً؟

٢  ______________

٣ 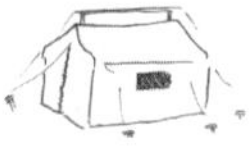 ______________

٤  ______________

٥  ______________

٦  ______________

## In summary

- Yes/no questions can be made by adding a question marker (هل or أ) to a statement. Question markers are not generally used in less formal Arabic, with the tone of voice being used to convey a question.
- Other questions can be formed by putting specific question words such as أين؟ ayna? or كيف؟ kayfa? in front of a sentence without changing the word order: كيفَ ذهبتَ إلى مصر؟ kayfa dhahabta ilā miṣr? (How did you go to Egypt?).
- كم؟ kam? (how many?) is followed by a *singular* noun (written with an extra alif if it has no ة): كم بيتاً؟ kam baytan (how many houses?).

unit 10

# Possession: iḍafa (إضافة) and attached pronouns

To express possession, as in 'Anwar's book' or 'the manager of the company', Arabic puts two or more nouns directly together in the order *possessed + possessor*:

| | |
|---|---|
| Anwar's book | كتاب أنوَر kitāb anwar |
| Mohammed's son | ابن محمّد ibn muḥammad |
| the door of the house | باب البيت bāb al-bayt |

This type of construction is known as إضافة iḍāfa, literally meaning 'addition'.

Only the *final* noun in an iḍāfa can have the article ال al-:

| | |
|---|---|
| the son of the manager | ابن المدير<br>ibn al-mudīr |
| the son of the manager of the department | ابن مدير القِسم<br>ibn mudīr al-qism |
| the son of the manager of the sales department ('department of sales') | ابن مدير قسم المُبيعات<br>ibn mudīr qism al-mubīɛāt |

The meaning will change if the last noun is indefinite:

| | |
|---|---|
| the manager of a department | مدير قسم mudīr qism |
| the door of a house | باب بيت bāb bayt |

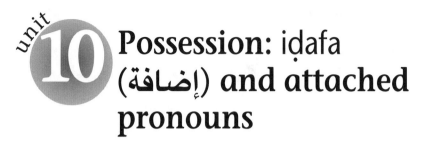

## Feminine words in iḍāfa

If the first word in an iḍāfa ends with ة a (tā' marbūṭa), the 't' is pronounced:

| | | |
|---|---|---|
| Anwar's car | سيّارة أنور | sayyārat̲ anwar |
| Mohammed's wife | زوجة محمّد | zawjat̲ muḥammad |
| the village school | مدرسة القَرية | madrasat̲ al-qarya |

### *Activity 1*

Look at the pictures of Anwar and Zainab surrounded by their possessions. Make sentences, as in the examples.

هذا كلب أنور.
(hadhā kalb anwar.)

هذه درّاجة زينب.
(hadhihi darrājat zaynab.)

## Plurals in iḍāfa

Generally, plural words can be put into possessive iḍāfa in the same way as singular words:

| | | |
|---|---|---|
| the president's cars | سيّارات الرّئيس | sayyārāt ar-ra'īs |
| bottles of cola | زجاجات كولا | zujājāt kūlā |

However, the sound masculine plural ون ūn/ين īn ending, as in مدرّسون/مدرّسين mudarrisūn/mudarrisīn (teachers), changes when in an iḍāfa:

- If the SMP is the *first* word in an iḍāfa, it loses the final ن n, but it may be either و ū or ي ī depending on the sentence (see Case Notes for more detail).
- If the SMP is the *final* word in an iḍāfa, the ين īn ending is always used.

| | |
|---|---|
| Where are the boy's teachers? | أينَ مدرّسو الولد؟<br>ayna mudarrisū l-walad? |
| I spoke to the company's accountants. | كَلَّمتُ محاسبي الشركة.<br>kallamtu muḥāsibī sh-sharika. |
| I went to the office of the engineers. | ذَهَبتُ إلى مكتب المهندسين.<br>dhahabtu ilā maktab al-muhandisīn |

## Adjectives and iḍāfa

As a rule, you can't separate words in an iḍāfa, so any adjective will come at the end even if it describes the first word. The adjective will match the gender of the noun it is describing and will have the article الـ al- if the noun is definite:

| | |
|---|---|
| the town's beautiful river | نهر المدينة الجميل<br>nahr al-madīna al-jamīl |
| the beautiful town's river | نهر المدينة الجميلة<br>nahr al-madīna al-jamīla |
| the small boy's bicycle | درّاجة الولد الصغير<br>darrārajat al-walad aṣ-ṣaghīr |
| the boy's small bicycle | درّاجة الولد الصغيرة<br>darrārajat al-walad aṣ-ṣaghīra |

### Activity 2

Form iḍāfa contructions for these English possessive phrases, as in the example

| | | |
|---|---|---|
| 1 | Ahmed's new car | سيّارة أحمد الجديدة |
| 2 | Jihan's old pen | ……………… |
| 3 | the engineers of the factory | ……………… |
| 4 | the boy's heavy bag | ……………… |
| 5 | Mohammed's white shirt | ……………… |
| 6 | the bakers of the town | ……………… |
| 7 | the window of the small house | ……………… |
| 8 | the company of the Iraqi engineers | ……………… |

## Case Notes

You have met the genitive case used with prepositions of place in Unit 8. The genitive case is also used for possession.

The *second* noun in an idāfa (and any subsequent nouns) will have the genitive case ending, -*(t)in* for an indefinite noun, or -*(t)i* for a definite noun, while the case of the first noun will vary depending on the sentence:

| | |
|---|---|
| This is the door of the house. | هذا بابُ البيتِ.<br>hādhā bāb*u* l-bayt*i*. |
| He opened the door of the house. | فتَحَ بابَ البيتِ.<br>fataḥa bāb*a* l-bayt*i*. |
| She's the manager of a company. | هي مديرةُ شَرِكةٍ.<br>hiya mudīra*tu* sharika*tin*. |
| We sat next to the manager of a company. | جلسنا بجانب مديرةِ شَرِكةٍ.<br>jalasnā bi-jānib mudīra*ti* sharika*tin* |

**Sound masculine plural**

In the accusative and genitive cases, the ون -ūn ending of the SMP changes to ين -īn. Therefore the ين -īn ending is used for the second noun in an idāfa or after a positional word:

| | |
|---|---|
| the office of the engineers | مكتبُ المهندسين<br>maktab*u* l-muhandis*īn* |
| I sat next to the teachers. | جَلَستُ بجانب المدرّسين.<br>jalastu bi-jānib al-mudarris*īn.* |

When the SMP is the *first* noun in an iḍāfa, the case ending will vary depending on the sentence. In addition, the ن n is dropped:

| | |
|---|---|
| Where are the boy's teachers? | أينَ مدرّسو الولدِ؟<br>ayna mudarris*ū* l-walad*i*? |
| I sat next to the boy's teachers. | جَلَستُ بجانب مدرّسي الولدِ.<br>jalastu bi-jānib mudarris*ī* l-walad*i.* |

## Attached pronouns

The Arabic equivalent of 'my', 'your', 'his', etc. are *endings* attached to the word being referred to: كتابي kitāb*ī* (*my* book); بيتنا bayt(u)*nā* (*our* house). The main attached endings are:

| | |
|---|---|
| my | ـي ī |
| your *(masc.)* | ـك -ka (-ak) |
| your *(fem.)* | ـك -ki (-ik) |
| his | ـه -hu (-uh) |
| her | ـها -hā |
| our | ـنا -nā |
| your *(pl.)* | ـكُم -kum |
| their *(masc.)* | ـهُم -hum |
| their *(fem.)* | ـهُنَّ -hunna |

In more formal Arabic, possessive endings other than ـي ī (my) should be preceded by a vowel representing the appropriate case ending (see Case Notes panels). However, in a less formal context, alternative pronunciations are used which avoid having to take account of these case endings. These are given in brackets in the examples below. Compare the formal pronunciation with the informal in brackets:

| | |
|---|---|
| your *(masc.)* book | كتابك kitāb<u>uka</u> (kitāb<u>ak</u>) |
| your *(fem.)* house | بيتك bayt<u>uki</u> (bayt<u>ik</u>) |
| Where's his office? | أين مكتبه؟ ayna maktab<u>uhu</u> (maktab<u>uh</u>)? |
| She's in her house. | هي في بيتها hiya fī bayt<u>ihā</u> (bayt<u>hā</u>) |

As a learner you can choose to use the informal, while recognising the formal pronunciation.

As with iḍāfa, the ة is pronounced when an attached pronoun is added. It will also be spelt as a regular ت:

| | |
|---|---|
| his car | سيّارته sayyāratuhu (sayyāratuh) |
| our bag | حقيبتنا ḥaqībatunā (ḥaqībatnā) |
| their school | مدرستهم madrasatuhum (madrasathum) |

In formal Arabic, ـه -hu (his) and ـهُم/ـهُنَّ -hum/-hunna (their) change to -hi and -him/-hinna after the sound i or ay:

| | |
|---|---|
| in his car | في سيّارته fī sayyārati*hi* |
| They went to their house. | ذَهبوا إلى بيتِهِم. dhahabū ilā bayti*him* |
| They went to it. | ذَهَبوا إليه. dhahabū ilay*hi* |

### *Activity 3*

Put the correct possessive ending on the nouns, as in the example. Use the informal or formal pronunciation as you prefer.

١ بيت + هو = **بيته** baytuhu (baytuh)

٢ مدرسة + هم = ______

٣ حال + أنتَ = ______

٤ قلم + هي = ______

٥ سيّارة + أنا = ______

٦ مدينة + نحن = ______

٧ كلب + أنتِ = ______

٨ بيت + أنتم= ______

### *Activity 4*

Make sentences using possessive endings, as in the example. Use the informal or formal pronunciation as you prefer.

١ أنا في بيت نادية. **أنا في بيتها.** anā fī baytihā (baythā)

٢ هل هذا كتاب أحمد؟ ______

٣ لا، هذا كتاب زينب. ______

٤ سيّارات المدرّسين في الشارع. ______

٥ باب البيت أبيض. ______

٦ أين حقيبة الممرّضات؟ ______

٧ مكتب المهندسين الكبير قريب من المدرسة.

______

٨ كيف حال زوجك؟ ______

## Ownership

The Arabic prepositions لِـ li- (for/belonging to), عِنْدَ ʿinda (at/*chez*) and مع maʿa (with) are used with a noun or possessive ending to express the equivalent of 'to have'. لِـ li- and عِنْدَ ʿinda express general ownership, whereas مع maʿa implies you have the thing *with you:*

| | |
|---|---|
| I have a brother. | عَندي أخ. ʿindī akh. |
| Fatima has a large car. | لِفاطمة سيّارة كبيرة.<br>li-faṭima sayyāra kabīra. |
| Do you have a pen [with you]? | هل معك قلم؟<br>hal maʿak qalam? |

Notice that لِـ li-, like all other one-letter Arabic words, is written joined to the word following. The vowel changes to لَـ la- before the possessive pronouns هُ -hu (his), ها -hā (her) and هُم -hum (their):

| | |
|---|---|
| She has a black dog. | لَها كلب أسود.<br>lahā kalb aswad. |
| They have a house in France. | لَهم بيت في فرنسا.<br>lahum bayt fī faransā. |

### *Activity 5*

Join the Arabic to the equivalent English, for example a) ٦.

| | |
|---|---|
| *a) I have an aunt whose name is May.* | ١ لأمّي سيّارة جديدة. |
| *b) Do you have a dog?* | ٢ لنا ابنة وابن. |
| *c) Does he have a dog?* | ٣ هل معك الكتاب؟ |
| *d) We have a daughter and a son.* | ٤ هل عندك كلب؟ |
| *e) Do you have the book?* | ٥ للمهندسين مكتب كبير. |
| *f) My mother has a new car.* | ٦ لي خالة اسمها ماي. |
| *g) The engineers have a large office.* | ٧ هل عنده كلب؟ |

## Case Notes

Nouns with a possessive ending are definite and will carry the appropriate case ending in formal Arabic:

| | |
|---|---|
| our house | بيتُنا bayt*u*nā |
| in our house | في بيتِنا bayt*i*nā |
| his car | سيّارتُه sayyārat*u*hu |
| under his car | تحت سيّارتِه taḥt sayyārat*i*hi |

The sound masculine plural loses the final ن when a possessive ending is added, as it does in iḍafa constructions:

| | |
|---|---|
| the bank and its accountants | البنك ومحاسبوهُ<br>al-bank wa muḥāsibūhu |
| We are with our teachers. | نحن مع مدرّسينا.<br>naḥnu maɛa mudarrisīnā. |

## In summary

- Arabic puts two or more nouns directly together in the order *possessed* + *possessor* to express possession, e.g. بيت النجّار bayt an-najjār (the carpenter's house). This type of possessive construction is called إضافة iḍāfa.
- Only the last word in an إضافة iḍāfa can have ال al, even though the first noun is definite.
- Endings are added to Arabic nouns to convey the meaning of 'my', 'your', etc.: بيتي baytī (my house).
- لِـ li-, عِنْد ɛinda and مع maɛa can be used with nouns or possessive endings to express ownership: لِمحمّد سيّارة غالية li-muḥammad sayyāra ghālya (Mohammed has an expensive car).

unit 11

# Plurals: broken plural

Remember that there are two basic types of Arabic plural:

- sound plural (الجمع السالم al-jamع as-sālim):
  *sound masculine plural* (SMP) -ūn/-īn: مدرّس mudarris (teacher) → مدرّسون/مدرّسين mudarrisūn/mudarrisīn (teachers)
  *sound feminine plural* (SFP) -āt: سيّارة sayyāra (car) → سيّارات sayyārāt (cars)
- broken plural (جمع التكسير jamع at-taksīr), formed by changing the internal vowels of the singular word, similar to the way English turns 'mouse' into 'mice' or 'man' into 'men'.

Unit 5 explained how the sound plural is formed. This unit will look at broken plurals.

## Forming broken plurals

Many basic Arabic nouns cannot be made plural using either the SMP or SFP. They are made plural by using the *broken plural* (جمع التكسير jamع at-taksīr). Although this system may at first seem random, there is method in the 'breakage'.

To form a broken plural you need to identify the (usually) three root consonants of a noun (see Unit 1). This can often be done by ignoring long and short vowels and any ة (tā' marbūṭa):

كَلب kalb (dog) → root = ك / ل / ب

صاحِب ṣāḥib (friend/owner) → root = ص / ح / ب

عُلبة عulba (box/packet) → root = ع / ل / ب

The root letters, always in the same sequence, are then put into a number of different patterns to form plurals:

كَلب kalb (dog) → كِلاب kilāb (dogs)

صاحِب ṣāḥib (friend/owner) → أصحاب aṣḥāb (friends/owners)

عُلبة ɛulba (box/packet) → عُلَب ɛulab (boxes/packets)

You can see that the plural of كَلب kalb (dog) takes the root letters and adds a kasra (i) after the first root letter ك and a long ā between the second and third root letters (ل and ب) to produce كِلاب kilāb (dogs). This plural pattern is known as the فِعال fiɛāl pattern in Arabic grammar, with the consonants ف / ع / ل representing the three root letters. (The root ف / ع / ل carries the meaning of 'to do' or 'to make' and this is why it is used in Arabic grammar to represent the generic root.) So, the pattern used to produce the plural أصحاب aṣḥāb (friends/owners) is known as the أفعال afɛāl pattern and the pattern used to produce عُلَب ɛulab (packets) as the فُعَل fuɛal pattern.

There are a dozen or so significant broken plural patterns. At the beginning you will need to learn each noun with its individual plural, although later you will begin to develop an instinct for which pattern to use.

For the sake of convenience, we have devided the patterns into groups, starting with some of the most common.

## Broken plurals: group 1

| Plural pattern | Example |
|---|---|
| فِعال fiɛāl | كَلب kalb (dog) → كِلاب kilāb |
| أفعال afɛāl | صاحِب ṣāḥib (friend/owner) → أصحاب aṣḥāb |
| فُعَل fuɛal | عُلبة ɛulba (box/packet) → عُلَب ɛulab |
| فُعول fuɛūl | بيت bayt (house) → بُيوت buyūt |

### *Activity 1*

Complete the chart below, using the appropriate plural pattern.

| Plural pattern | Plural | Singular |
|---|---|---|
| فُعول fuعūl | ١ ______ | بَنك bank (bank) |
| أفعال afعāl | ٢ ______ | وَلَد walad (boy) |
| ٣ ______ | صُوَر ṣuwar (pictures) | صورة ṣūra (picture) |
| فُعول fuعūl | ٤ ______ | قَصر qaṣr (palace) |
| ٥ ______ | أفلام aflām (films) | فيلم fīlm (film) |
| فِعال fiعāl | ٦ ______ | جَبَل jabal (mountain) |
| ٧ ______ | لُعَب luعab (toys) | لُعبة luعba (toy) |
| ٩ ______ | جِمال jimāl (camels) | ٨ ______ |
| ١١ ______ | مُلوك mulūk (kings) | ١٠ ______ |
| أفعال afعāl | ١٢ ______ | هَرَم haram (pyramid) |
| ١٤ ______ | شُيوخ shuyūkh (sheiks) | ١٣ ______ |

## Broken plurals: group 2

| Plural pattern | Example |
|---|---|
| فُعُل fuعul | كِتاب kitāb (book) → كُتُب kutub |
| أفعُل afعul | شَهر shahr (month) → أشهُر ash-hur |
| فَواعِل fawāعil | شارِع shāriع (street) → شَوارِع shawāriع |
| فُعَلاء fuعalā' | وزير wazīr (minister) → وُزَراء wuzarā' |

### *Activity 2*

Match the singular to the plural, for example: ١(g) .

| | |
|---|---|
| ١ سَهم (company share) | (a) سُفُن |
| ٢ مَدينة (town/city) | (b) رُؤَساء |
| ٣ طَريق (road/way) | (c) مُدُن |
| ٤ خاتِم (ring) | (d) طُرُق |
| ٥ سَفير (ambassador) | (e) أُمراء |
| ٦ رَئيس (president) | (f) مَوائِد |
| ٧ عاصِمة (capital city) | (g) أَسهُم |
| ٨ أمير (prince/emir) | (h) خَواتِم |
| ٩ سَفينة (ship) | (i) عَواصِم |
| ١٠ مائِدة (table) | (j) سُفَراء |

Now cover up the left-hand column and try to say plurals out loud after the singular.

## Other broken plurals

There are other broken plural patterns, such as قُمصان qumṣān, the plural of قميص qamīṣ (shirt), or خِيام khiyām, the plural of خيمة khayma (tent). These are best learnt as and when you encounter them.

A few words have four root letters (see Unit 1) and the plurals of these words tend to be similar to the فَواعِل fawāɛil pattern: فُندُق funduq (hotel) → فنادِق fanādiq (hotels).

## Using broken plurals in sentences

Don't forget that only humans are treated as plural in Arabic grammar. The plural of non-human objects and ideas is treated as feminine singular:

| Singular | Plural |
|---|---|
| هو وزير. huwa wazīr.<br>(He's a [gov.] minister.) | هُم وزراء. hum wuzarā'<br>(They are ministers.) |
| هو كتابي. huwa kitābī.<br>(It's my book.) | هي كُتُبي. hiya kutubī.<br>(They are my books.) |
| هذا وزير عراقيّ.<br>hādhā wazīr ᶓirāqī.<br>(This is an Iraqi minister.) | هؤلاء وُزَراء عراقيّون.<br>hā'ulā' wuzarā' ᶓirāqīyyūn.<br>(These are Iraqi ministers.) |
| هذا الخاتم مُستَورَد.<br>hādhā khātim mustawrad.<br>(This ring is imported.) | هذه الخواتم مُستَورَدة.<br>hādhihi l-khawātim mustawrada.<br>(These rings are imported.) |

## *Activity 3*

Make these sentences plural, as in the example:

١ هذا القَصر جميل. **هذه القصور جميلة.**

٢ السيّارة في الشارع. ..........

٣ اللُعبة بِجانِب الكتاب. ..........

٤ أين قَلَمي الجديد؟ ..........

٥ هناك جبل طويل. ..........

٦ بيتنا أبيض. ..........

٧ المدرّس مصريّ. ..........

٨ الهَرَم في الجيزة. ..........

٩ الكتاب القديم على المائدة. ..........

١٠ هذه صورة زينب. ..........

## Case Notes

Case endings can be added to plural nouns in much the same way as to singular nouns:

| | |
|---|---|
| house | بيتٌ bayt*un* |
| houses | بيوتٌ buyūt*un* |
| in the town | في المدينةِ fi l-madīna*ti* |
| in the towns | في المدنِ fi l-mudun*i* |

Exceptions are a few plural patterns which don't have tanwīn (*nunation*) in the indefinite, e.g.

| | |
|---|---|
| فَواعِلُ fawāɛil*u* | خواتمُ khawātim*u* (rings) |
| | الخواتمُ al-khawātim*u* (the rings) |
| فُعَلاءُ fuɛalā'*u* | وُزَراءُ wuzarā'*u* (ministers) |
| | الوُزَراءُ al-wuzarā'*u* (the ministers) |

**Optional Activity**

Write the case endings on your answers to Activity 3 and read the sentences out loud, e.g:

hādhihi l-quṣūr*u* jamīla*tun*. ١ هذه القصورُ جميلةٌ .

## In summary

- Many Arabic words are made plural using internal 'broken' plurals rather than external 'sound' plurals.
- Broken plurals are made by putting the root letters of singular nouns into different plural patterns.
- There are a dozen or so common broken plural patterns. The plural of individual words cannot easily be predicted by a beginner although certain patterns will emerge.

unit 12

# Comparative and superlative

The comparative and superlative are used to compare objects or ideas. The comparative in English is formed using *-er* with shorter adjectives or *more* with longer ones: fast*er*, *more* comfortable; the superlative using *-est* or *most*: fast*est*, *most* comfortable. Similarly, Arabic has a different method of forming the comparative and superlative with short, basic adjectives and longer, more complicated ones.

## Forming the comparative

Arabic forms the comparative in one of two ways:

### *1* أفعَل afعal *pattern*

The أفعَل afعal pattern is used with short, basic adjectives with three identifiable root letters. An alif is added before the first root letter and a fatḥa (a) between the second and third root letters:

> كبير kabīr (big) → أكبَر akbar (bigger)
>
> جميل jamīl (beautiful) → أجمَل ajmal (more beautiful)
>
> طويل ṭawīl (long/tall) → أطوَل aṭwal (longer/taller)

Some adjectives share the same second and third root letter (see Unit 1). These are written together in the comparative with the fatḥa (a) moving after the first root letter:

> جديد jadīd (new) → أجَدّ ajadd (newer)
>
> شَديد shadīd (strong) → أشَدّ ashadd (stronger)

If the final root of the adjective is ي or و, this changes to alif maqṣūra (ā written as ى) at the end of the comparative:

> غنيّ ghanī (rich) → أغنى aghnā (richer)
>
> حلو ḥilw (sweet) → أحلى aḥlā (sweeter)

## 2 أكثَر akthar + *noun*

Longer adjectives cannot generally be made into a comparative using the أفعل afʿal pattern. Instead أكثَر akthar (more) is used with a noun carrying the special tanwīn al-fatḥ (ـً -an) ending we have already met after كم؟ kam (see pages 50–2). Remember that this ending carries the meaning of 'as to' or 'regarding' and is written on an extra alif (اً) if the noun does *not* end in ta' marbūṭa:

> أكثر إفادةً akthar ifādatan (more useful – 'more as to usefulness')
>
> أكثر انتشاراً akthar intishāran (more widespread)
>
> أكثر ملائمةً akthar mulā'imatan (more suitable)

As a beginner, it is enough to recognise this. Later you will be able to form similar comparisons using the appropriate noun.

### *Activity 1*

Make these adjectives comparative, as in the example.

١ قبيح (ugly) ........أقبَح

٢ صغير (small) ..........

٣ قصير (short) ..........

٤ خفيف (light) ..........

٥ ثقيل (heavy) ..........

٦ قديم (old) ..........

٧ كثير (many) ..........

٨ سريع (fast) ..........

## Comparing things

The comparative doesn't generally change for masculine feminine or plural. The equivalent of *than* as in *bigger than* is من min (literally 'from'):

| | |
|---|---|
| The palace is older than the mosque. | القصر أقدم من المسجد.<br>al-qaṣr aqdam min al-masjid. |
| This car is faster than that car. | هذه السيّارة أسرع من تلك السيّارة.<br>hādhihi s-sayyāra asraع min tilka s-sayyāra. |
| My house is bigger than your house. | بيتي أكبر من بيتك.<br>baytī akbar min baytak (baytika). |

The attached pronouns, as used for possession (see Unit 10), can also be used with من min:

| | |
|---|---|
| I'm taller than her. | أنا أطول منها.<br>anā aṭwal minhā. |
| They're faster than us. | هم أسرع منّا.<br>hum asraع minnā. |

### *Activity 2*

Mine's better than yours! Use the comparative to do a bit of boasting, as in the examples.

أنا طويل. ← أنا أطول منك!
*I'm tall.* *I'm taller than you!*

سيّارتي سريعة. ← سيّارتي أسرع من سيّارتك!
*My car is fast.* *My car is faster than your car!*

١ بيتي قديم. ____________

٢ أنا غنيّ. ____________

٣ مدينتي جميلة. ____________

٤ حقيبتي خفيفة. ____________

٥ قميصي جديد. ____________

٦ أنا سريع. ____________

٧ سيّارتي غالية. ____________

٨ خاتمي كبير. ____________

## *Activity 3*

Now make as many sentences as you can comparing the teacher and the accountant in the picture, as in the examples:

المدرّس أطول من المحاسب.
al-mudarris aṭwal min al-muḥāsib.
*The teacher is taller than the accountant.*

بيت المحاسب أكبر من بيت المدرّس.
bayt al-muḥāsib akbar min bayt al-mudarris.
*The accountant's house is bigger than the teacher's house.*

## The superlative

The most common ways in Arabic to express a superlative, as in 'the fastest' or 'the most beautiful', is either to put the comparative in front of the noun:

أسرع سيّارة asraع sayyāra (the fastest car)

أجمل نهر ajmal nahr (the most beautiful river)

or simply to add the article الـ al to the comparative with the meaning 'the fastest one', 'the most beautiful one', etc:

الأسرع al-asraع

الأجمل al-ajmal

### *Activity 4*

Choose a phrase from the box to fill the gaps in the sentences.

| | | |
|---|---|---|
| أقدم بيت | أكبر مدينة | الأقصر |
| أسرع ولد | الأثقل | أجدّ مهندس |

١ محمود ________ في المدرسة.

٢ هل هذه الحقيبة خفيفة؟ لا، هي ________.

٣ هذا ________ في الشارع.

٤ القاهرة ________ في مصر.

٥ أمي أقصر مني ولكن أخي هو ________.

٦ بَدر ________ في المصنع.

## Case Notes

The accusative indefinite ending -*(t)an* is added to the noun when it is used in the structure أكثَر akthar (more) + noun. This means the extra alif tanwīn will appear if the noun does not end with ة taa marbūṭa (see Case Notes, Unit 9):

أكثر إفادةً akthar ifāda*tan* (more useful)

أكثر انتشاراً akthar intishār*an* (more widespread)

The superlative, e.g. أسرع ولد asraع walad (the fastest boy), is an إضافة iḍāfa structure (see Unit 10). So the second noun will have the genitive ending -*(t)in*:

أسرعُ ولدٍ asraع*u* walad*in* (fastest boy)

أرخصُ جريدةٍ arkhaṣ*u* jarīda*tin* (cheapest newspaper)

## In summary

- Arabic has a special comparative form: أفعَل afعal, e.g. أكبر akbar (bigger).
- من min is used to compare two things, e.g.: أكبر من... akbar min... (bigger than...).
- Longer adjectives that can't be put into the أفعَل afعal pattern are made comparative by using أكثر akthar (more) + noun with ـً (t)an: أكثر إفادةً akthar ifādatan (more useful).
- أفعَل afعal + (indefinite) noun = superlative (the -est/most): أكبر بيت akbar bayt (the biggest house).

unit 13

# The dual

Arabic grammar regards the plural as referring to three or more. There is a special dual form when referring to two. The dual ending ان/ـَين -ān/-ayn is added to a noun to express the meaning of 'two'.

كتاب kitāb (book)

كتابان/كتابَين kitābān/kitābayn (two books)

كُتُب kutub (three or more books)

The context will dictate whether the ان -ān or ـَين -ayn ending is used, in a similar way to the sound masculine plural alternative endings ون -ūn/ين -īn. (Note that spoken dialects generally use the ـَين -ayn dual ending in *all* contexts.)

If a word ends with ة tā marbūṭa this is pronounced when the dual ending is added:

مدينة madīna (town)

مدينتان/مدينتَين madīnatān/madīnatayn (two towns)

مُدُن mudun (three or more towns)

The dual is often used when talking about parts of the body, as many of these come in pairs:

| | |
|---|---|
| رِجل rijl (leg) | رِجلان/رِجلَين rijlān/rijlayn (two legs) |
| يَد yad (hand) | يَدان/يَدَين yadān/yadayn (two hands) |

## *Activity 1*

Make the dual to match the pictures, as in the example.

حقيبتان/حقيبتين (ḥaqībatān/ḥaqībatayn)

١  ______________

٢  ______________

٣  ______________

٤  ______________

٥  ______________

٦ 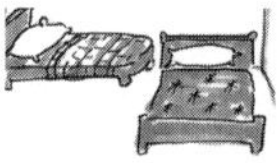 ______________

٧  ______________

٨ 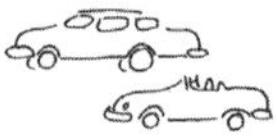 ______________

## Dual pronouns

The dual also has its own pronouns (and verbal forms which are covered in Part 2). Unlike the dual noun ending, this is a feature of Standard Arabic but rarely used in spoken dialects.

Dual pronouns are similar to the plural, but with a long ā:

| | |
|---|---|
| you (two) | أنتما antumā |
| they (two) | هما humā |

## The dual in sentences

The main uses of the final dual يْن -ayn ending are:

- when the dual noun is *after* a positional word or preposition
- when the dual noun is the *last* word in an iḍāfa
- when the dual noun is the *object* of a verb (see Unit 14).

Otherwise the ان -ān ending is generally used, although you should be aware there are exceptions to this.

| | |
|---|---|
| They are the two ambassadors. | هما السفيران.<br>humā s-safīrān. |
| I'm in front of the two houses. | أنا أمام البيتين.<br>anā amāma l-baytayn. |
| My sister bought two books from the market. | اشترت أختي كتابين من السوق.<br>ishtarat ukhtī kitābayn min s-sūq. |
| This is the office of the two engineers | هذا مكتب المهندسَين.<br>hādhā maktab al-muhandisayn. |
| Where are her two daughters? | أين بنتاها؟<br>ع ayn bintāhā? |
| Both the schools of the town are large. | مدرستا المدينة كبيرتان.<br>madrasatā l-madīna kabīratān. |

Notice that when the dual is the *first* word in an iḍāfa or has a possessive ending, it loses the final ن (n) in a similar way to the sound masculine plural.

## Case Notes

The dual case endings are comparable to the sound masculine plural (see Units 5 and 10). As with the the sound masculine plural, the dual is one of the few instances when the case ending is written as part of the main script.

The ان -ān ending is *nominative* and the ـَين -ayn ending is *accusative* and *genitive.* As the accusative is used for the object of a verb and the genitive is used after positional words and for the last word in an iḍāfa, the ـَين -ayn ending is used in these contexts.

## *Activity 2*

What do these sentences mean? Match the Arabic to the equivalent English.

| | |
|---|---|
| a) I found the two boys behind the door. | ١ هناك زجاجتان تحت المائدة. |
| b) My clothes are in the two bags. | ٢ مُنى عندها سيّارة ودرّاجتان. |
| c) They are the two Saudi engineers. | ٣ وَجَدتُ الولدين وراء الباب. |
| d) There are two bottles under the table. | ٤ أحمد مع والِدَيه. |
| e) Mona has a car and two bikes. | ٥ هما المهندسان السَعوديّان. |
| f) Ahmed is with his parents. | ٦ مَلابِسي في الحقيبتين. |

## In summary

- Arabic has a special dual ending used when referring to two items or two people.
- The ending ان -ān or ـَين -ayn is added to the noun: بيتان/البيتَين baytān/baytayn (two houses).
- The dual ending loses the final ن n when it is the first noun in an iḍāfa: بيتا الملك baytā l-malik (the king's two houses).

part 2

# Arabic verbs

# unit 14 Past verbs

Arabic sentences can be either verbal or non-verbal. It is possible to express many basic concepts without using a verb:

| | |
|---|---|
| We are in the bank. | نحن في البنك.<br>naḥnu fī l-bank. |
| My mother is in school with my brother. | أمي في المدرسة مع أخي.<br>ummī fī l-madrasa maɛa akhī. |
| This chair is very old. | هذا الكرسي قديم جدّاً.<br>hāhdā l-kursī qadīm jiddan. |
| The ministers have a meeting tomorrow. | لِلوُزَراء اجتماع غداً.<br>lil-wuzarā' ijtimāɛ ghadan. |

To go beyond this type of elementary statement, however, you need to understand how the Arabic verb system works.

There are only two basic tenses in Arabic:

- الماضي al-māḍī (*past*)
- المُضارع al-muḍāriɛ (*imperfect*, used to express the present and future)

Grammatically, it makes sense to begin with the past tense as it is simpler.

## Basic verbs in the past tense (singular)

Verbs are categorised into *basic* and *derived* forms. Basic verbs are 'no frills' verbs generally based around three root consonants (see Unit 1). Derived forms manipulate the root consonants, adding extra letters before and between them, to create different but related meanings. Units 14–16 will present basic verbs in the two tenses; Unit 17 will cover the derived forms.

The هُوَ huwa (he/it *masc.*) past tense shows the verb in its simplest form:

| | | |
|---|---|---|
| He found the key. | وَجَدَ المِفتاح. | wajada l-miftāḥ. |
| He opened the door. | فَتَحَ الباب. | fataḥa l-bāb. |

The three root letters of the verb are each followed by a short fatḥa (a) vowel. If we remove the final -a and add the ending تُ -tu, the verb will then refer to أنا anā (I):

| | | |
|---|---|---|
| I found the key. | وَجَدتُ المِفتاح. | wajadtu l-miftāḥ. |
| I opened the door. | فَتَحتُ الباب. | fataḥtu l-bāb. |

You do not have to use the pronoun أنا anā or هُوَ huwa since the ending of the verb will tell you who is carrying out the action.

Here are all the singular endings for past verbs:

| *example* | *ending* | |
|---|---|---|
| (I opened) fataḥtu فَتَحتُ | -tu تُ | I أنا |
| (you *m.* opened) fataḥta فَتَحتَ | -ta تَ | you *(m.)* أنتَ |
| (you *f.* opened) fataḥti فَتَحتِ | -ti تِ | you *(f.)* أنتِ |
| (he/it opened) fataḥa فَتَحَ | -a ـَ | he/it هو |
| (she/it opened) fataḥat فَتَحَت | -at ـَت | she/it هي |

You may have noticed that all the singular past verbs except فتح fataḥa are spelt the same – فتحت – and only distinguished by the short vowels that are not usually written in modern Arabic. When reading Arabic without vowels you will need to pay close attention to the context to decide on the meaning and pronunciation.

The common part of the past tense that appears before the individual endings is the 'stem'. This is usually vowelled with two fatḥas: فَتَح fataḥ (opened), وَجَد wajad (found). However, sometimes the second vowel is a kasra: شَرِب sharib (drank), سَمِع samiع (heard).

## Activity 1

Use one of the verbs in the box with the appropriate ending to fill in the gaps in the sentences, as in the example:

| | | |
|---|---|---|
| ذَهَب dhahab *(went)* | شَرِب sharib *(drunk)* | فَتَح fataḥ *(opened)* |
| جَلَس jalas *(sat)* | وَجَد wajad *(found)* | سَمِع samiع *(heard)* |

١ (أنا) ذَهَبتُ ........ إلى البنك.

٢ (هي) ........ على الكرسي.

٣ هل (أنتَ) ........ المفتاح؟

٤ (هو) ........ الكولا.

٥ (هي) ........ إلى مكتبها.

٦ هل (أنتِ) ........ الخبر* في الراديو؟

٧ (أنا) ........ باب البيت بالمفتاح.

٨ (هو) ........ قطّة تحت سيّارته.

*الخبر al-khabar = *the news item*

## Word order

When the subject (the 'doer') of the verb is mentioned, it generally comes *after* the verb in Standard Arabic:
*verb + subject + rest of sentence*

| | |
|---|---|
| Fatima opened the door. | فتحَت فاطمة الباب.<br>fataḥat faṭima al-bāb. |
| The Prime Minister attended the exhibition. | حَضَرَ رئيس الوزراء المعرض.<br>ḥaḍara ra'īs al-wuzarā' al-maɛraḍ. |

### *Activity 2*

Sarah (سارة) is a teacher. What did she do yesterday (أمس ams)? Match the sentences with the pictures.

جلسَت على كرسي...

بعد الدرس حضرَت اجتماع المدرّسين...

ذهبَت الى الفَصل.

وشربَت فِنجان شاي.

سارة مدرّسة. ذهبَت أمس إلى المدرسة...

وجدَت سارة الكُتُب فوق المائدة.

ورَجَعَت (returned) الى بيتها.

وفتحَت باب المدرسة.

## *Activity 3*

Now imagine you are Sarah and give an account of your day yesterday:

أنا مدرّسة. ذَهَبتُ أمس إلى المدرسة...

## Basic verbs in the past tense (plural)

Here are the plural endings for the past tense. Remember that the plural forms are used *only* with people; non-human plurals take the feminine singular (هي hiya) form of the verb.

| | example | ending | |
|---|---|---|---|
| | (we opened) fataḥnā فَتَحنا | -nā نا | we نَحنُ |
| | (you *m. pl.* opened) fataḥtum فَتَحتُم | -tum تُم | you *(m. pl.)* أنتُم |
| | (you *f. pl.* opened) fataḥtunna فَتَحتُنَّ | -tunna تُنَّ | you *(f. pl.)* أنتُنَّ |
| | (they *m.* opened) fataḥū فَتَحوا | -ū وا | they *(m.)* هُم |
| | (they *f.* opened) fataḥna فَتَحنَ | -na نَ | they *(f.)* هُنَّ |

| | |
|---|---|
| We sat on the steps. | جَلَسنا على السُلَّم.<br>jalasna ɛalā s-sullam. |
| They *(m.)* attended the meeting. | حَضَروا الاجتماع.<br>ḥaḍarū l-ijtimāɛ. |
| You *(m. pl.)* heard the news yesterday. | سَمِعتُم الخَبَر أمس.<br>samiɛtum al-khabar ams. |

Note that there is a silent ا alif written after the و waw of the هُم form of the verb: فتحوا fataḥū. This is purely a spelling convention and is *not* pronounced. Don't confuse it with the extra (accusative) alif sometimes written on the end of nouns (e.g. وَلَداً waladan – see Unit 9).

As with pronouns, masculine plural verbs are more common since all members of a group need to be female for the feminine plural to be used. Learn the masculine first; the feminine plurals shaded in the table are mainly for recognition. There are also special verb endings for the dual. However, these verb endings are relatively uncommon and so will be covered later in Unit 20.

## Plural verbs in sentences

A quirk of Arabic grammar states that if a verb comes *before* a plural subject the verb will be singular, but if it comes *after* the subject it will be plural. This can mean a switch in mid-sentence:

> ذَهَبَ الأصحاب إلى النادي وشَرِبوا كولا.
> dhahaba l-aṣḥāb ilā n-nādī wa-sharibū kūlā.
> The friends went *(m. sing.)* to the club and drank *(m. pl.)* cola.

However, the verb will still be feminine if the subject is feminine:

> رَجَعَت البَنات إلى الفصل وجَلَسنَ على الكراسي.
> rajaعat al-banāt ilā l-faṣl wa-jalasna عala l-karāsī.
> The girls returned *(f. sing.)* to the classroom and sat *(f. pl.)* on the chairs.

Unsurprisingly given their complexity, most of these rules are ignored in everyday speech and the masculine plural often used throughout, even for females. As a learner you can get away with the same when you speak, but should be prepared to recognise the more correct standard versions and eventually to use them yourself in written and formal spoken Arabic.

## Questions

There is no special question form of the verb in Arabic. You can use the question marker هل hal or any of the other question words (see Unit 9) with the relevant part of the verb:

| | |
|---|---|
| Did you go to the bank? | هل ذهبتَ الى البنك؟<br>hal dhahabta ilā l-bank? |
| When did they go out? | متّى خرجوا؟ mattā kharajū? |
| Where did Ahmed hear the news? | أينَ سمع أحمد الخبر؟<br>ayna samiꜥa aḥmad al-khabar? |

### *Activity 4*

Make these sentences and questions plural, as in the example.

١ ذَهَبَ إلى المصنع. **ذَهَبوا إلى المَصنع.**

٢ خَرَجَ من البيت. ..........

٣ جلَستُ في المكتب. ..........

٤ هل سَمِعتَ الخبر؟ ..........

٥ حضَرَت الاجتماع. ..........

٦ أين وَجَدَ المدرّس مفتاح الباب؟ ..........

٧ ذَهَبتُ الى بيت أُختي. ..........

٨ فَتَحَ الولد الزُجاجة وشَرِبَ الكولا. ..........

### *Activity 5*

Say these out loud in Arabic and then write them down.

1 I went to the bank yesterday.
2 She drank a cup of coffee.
3 Did you *(masc. pl.)* find the key?
4 We attended the meeting in the factory.
5 Ahmed heard the news in the restaurant (المَطعَم al-maṭꜥam).
6 They *(masc.)* sat down next to the teacher.

## Case Notes

The subject ('doer') of a verb, if included, will have the *nominative* case ending. For the object ('receiver') of a verb, the *accusative* is used: *-an* for the indefinite (with the extra alif tanwīn اً if the noun does not end in ة) and *-a* for the definite:

| | |
|---|---|
| The minister attended a meeting. | حَضَرَ الوزيرُ اجتماعاً.<br>ḥaḍara l-wazīr*u* ijtimāꜥ*an*. |

He found the key. وَجَدَ المِفتاحَ. wajada l-miftāḥa.

You *(m. pl.)* heard the news yesterday. سَمِعتُم الخَبَرَ أمس. samiعtum al-khabara ams.

Remember that after a preposition, the genitive case endings are used (see Unit 8 Case Notes):

I went to the town. ذهبتُ الى المدينةِ. dhahabtu ilā l-madīnat*i* .

**Optional Activity**

Mark the case endings on these sentences and then read them out loud.

١ فَتَحنا الباب.

٢ وَجَدتُ الحَقيبة.

٣ وَجَدَ الولد كتابا في الشارِع.

٤ هل سَمِعتَ الخبر في المَطعَم؟

٥ حَضَرَت المدرّسة اجتماعا.

٦ شَرِبَ الرَجُل فنجان قهوة.

## In summary

- There are two basic tenses in Arabic: الماضي (past) and المُضارع (imperfect, used for present and future).
- The past tense of basic verbs is made up of a three-consonant stem with different endings showing the subject, e.g. فَتَحَ fataḥ*a* (*he* opened), فَتَحتُ fataḥ*tu* (*I* opened), فَتَحوا fataḥ*ū* (*they* opened).
- The verb often comes first in a sentence: فَتَحَت زينب الخزانة. fataḥat zaynab al-khazāna (Zaynab opened the safe).
- Plural verbs are only used with people. Non-human plurals use the feminine singular (هي) verb.

# unit 15 Present/future verbs

The second Arabic verbal tense is the *imperfect* or المُضارع al-muḍāriع, used for describing present and future events.

Like the past tense, the imperfect verb changes depending on the subject ('I', 'you', 'he', etc.). However, in the imperfect tense these changes are prefixes (letters on the beginning of the root stem), sometimes combined with endings. For example, يَشرَب *ya*shrab, means '*he* drinks'; this changes to تَشرَب *ta*shrab for '*she* drinks' and يَشربون *ya*shrab*ūna* for '*they* drink'. The common element is شرَب shrab which can be described as the 'stem' of the present tense. In this case, the three root letters are sh/r/b and there is a fatḥa (a) after the second root letter.

## Basic verbs in the present tense (singular)

Here are all the singular endings for present verbs, using the verb يَفتَح yaftaḥ (open):

| *example* | *ending* | *prefix* | |
|---|---|---|---|
| (I open) aftaḥ(u*) أفتَح | | a- أ | أنا |
| (you *m.* open) taftaḥ(u) تَفتَح | | ta- تَـ | أنتَ |
| (you *f.* open) taftaḥīna تَفتَحين | -īna ين | ta- تَـ | أنتِ |
| (he/it opens) yaftaḥ(u) يَفتَح | | ya- يَـ | هو |
| (she/it opens) taftaḥ(u) تَفتَح | | ta- تَـ | هي |

* *The full pronunciation includes a final u, but this is not heard except in formal contexts.*

Notice that the present verb for أنتَ (you *masc.*) is exactly the same as for هي (she/it).

The middle vowel in the present stem of basic verbs can change. The vowel can be:

- fatḥa, as in يفتَح yaft*a*ḥ (open),
- kasra, as in يغسِل yaghs*i*l (wash), or
- ḍamma, as in يسكُن yask*u*n (live).

| | |
|---|---|
| Every day she opens the safe. | كُلّ يوم تَفتَح الخزانة. kull yawm taftaḥ al-khazāna. |
| Do you *(m.)* go to school by car? | هل تَذهَب إلى المدرسة بالسيّارة؟ hal tadh-hab ilā l-madrasa bis-sayyāra? |
| I wash my face in the morning. | أغسِل وَجهي صباحاً. aghsil wajhī ṣabāḥan. |
| Where does he live? | أينَ يَسكُن؟ ayna yaskun? |

## *Activity 1*

Change these sentences to match the subject in brackets, as in the example.

١ (هُوَ) يَغسِل وجهه صباحاً. (هِي)

**تغسِل وجهها صباحاً.**

٢ (أنا) أسكُن في الكُويت. (هُوَ) ______

٣ تَشرَب كولا؟ (أنتِ) ______

٤ (هو) يَسكُن مَعَ أمّه. (أنا) ______

٥ متّى تَخرُجين من البيت؟ (أنتَ)

______

٦ يذهَب أنوَر إلى المكتب بالسيّارة. (زينب)

______

## Activity 2

Read about Nadia's routine below and fill in the gaps with one of the verbs from the box.

| | | | |
|---|---|---|---|
| *(plays)* تَلعَب | *(goes)* تَذهب | *(eats)* تأكُل | *(drinks)* تَشرَب |
| *(sits)* تَجلِس | *(lives)* تَسكُن | *(returns)* تَرجع | *(washes)* تَغسِل |

______ نادية في القاهرة. كلّ يوم ______ وجهها

و ______ طَبَق فول*. بَعدَ ذلك ______ إلى المدرسة

بالأتوبيس و ______ في الفَصل. ______ إلى

البيت الساعة الثالثة.

______ زجاجة كولا

و ______ مَعَ

أصحابها في

الحَديقة**.

*طَبَق فول *a plate of beans* = ṭabaq fūl

**حَديقة *park/garden* = ḥadīqa

Now imagine you are Nadia and change the routine to أنا anā (I). Start like this:

**أسكن في القاهرة ...**

## Basic verbs in the present tense (plural)

Here is the plural for present verbs. The shaded feminine plural is mainly for recognition. Learn the masculine plural first.

| example | ending | prefix | |
|---|---|---|---|
| (we open) naftaḥ(u) نَفتَح | | na- نَـ | نَحنُ |
| (you *m. pl.* open) taftaḥūna تَفتَحونَ | -ūna ونَ | ta- تَـ | أنتُم |
| (you *f. pl.* open) taftaḥna تَفتَحنَ | -na نَ | ta- تَـ | أنتُنَّ |
| (they *m.* open) yaftaḥūna يَفتَحونَ | -ūna ونَ | ya- يَـ | هُم |
| (they *f.* open) yaftaḥna يَفتَحنَ | -na نَ | ya- يَـ | هُنَّ |

Notice that the prefix for 'you' verbs is always تـ and the prefix for 'they' is يـ. The ending shows the gender and number: ون -ūna for masculine plural and ن -na for feminine plural.

| | |
|---|---|
| We attend a meeting every Thursday. | نحضر اجتماعاً كلّ يوم خميس.<br>naḥḍur ijtimāɛan kull yawm khamīs. |
| They *(masc.)* live in Baghdad. | يَسكُنونَ في بَغداد.<br>yaskunūna fī l-baghdād. |
| Do you *(masc. pl.)* drink coffee in the morning? | هل تَشربونَ قهوة صباحاً؟<br>hal tashrabūna qahwa ṣabāḥan? |
| On Friday my friends go to the restaurant and eat pizza. | يوم الجمعة يَذهب أصحابي الى المَطعَم ويأكُلونَ بيتزا.<br>yawm il-jumɛa yadh-hab aṣḥābī ilā l-maṭɛam wa-ya'kulūna bītzā. |

## *Activity 3*

Make these sentences plural, as in the example. Remember:
1 If the verb comes before the subject it will be singular.
2 Use a feminine *singular* verb (i.e. تَـ ta-) for non-human plurals.

١ يَغسِل السيّارة يوم الجمعة. **يَغسِلونَ السيّارة يوم الجمعة.**

٢ أسكُن في بغداد. ____________

٣ هل تَذهب إلى البنك؟ ____________

٤ يَذهب الولد إلى الحديقة ويلَعب تَنِس.

____________

٥ الكلب يَفتح الباب. ____________

٦ أرجَع من المكتَب وأشرَب فنجان شاي.

____________

## *Activity 4*

Complete these sentences describing what these people do and where they work. Use the verb يَعمَل yaعmal (to work) with the correct prefixes and endings. The first is an example.

١  هو **مدرّس ويَعمَل في مدرسة.**

٢  هي ____________

٣ 

هو ..............................

٤ 

هم ..............................

٥ 

هو طَبّاخ ..............................

٦ 

هم .............................. مَخبَز.

٧ 

هُنَّ .............................. مُستَشفى.

## Talking about the future

The imperfect is also used for talking about the future, often preceded by the future indicators سـَ sa- or سوف sawfa:

| | |
|---|---|
| We're going to the museum today. | سَنَذهَب الى المَتحف اليوم.<br>sa-nadh-hab ilā l-matḥaf al-yawm. |
| Ahmad is going to play tennis with Nadya. | سوف يلعَب أحمد التَنِس مَعَ نادية.<br>sawfa yalɛab aḥmad tanis maɛa nādiya. |

## Attached pronouns with verbs

The pronouns used on the end of nouns to describe possession, e.g. بيتها bayt(u)*hā* (*her* house), can also be used with verbs. (The vowels in brackets are pronounced in more formal Arabic.)

| | | |
|---|---|---|
| يَغسِلها يوم الجمعة. | ← | يَغسل السيّارة يوم الجمعة. |
| yaghsil(u)hā yawm al-jumعa. | ← | yaghsil as-sayyāra yawm al-jumعa. |
| *He washes it on Friday.* | ← | *He washes the car on Friday.* |
| سَأشرَبه في المساء. | ← | سَأشرَب العصير في المساء. |
| sa-ashrabuh(u) fī l-masā'. | ← | sa-ashrab al-عaṣīr fī l-masā'. |
| *I'll drink it in the evening.* | ← | *I'll drink the juice in the evening.* |
| سمِعناهم في الحديقة. | ← | سمِعنا الأطفال في الحديقة. |
| samiعnāhum fī l-ḥadīqa. | ← | samiعnā l-aTfāl fī l-ḥadīqa. |
| *We heard them in the park.* | ← | *We heard the children in the park.* |

The ending ـي -ī (my) changes to ـني -nī (me) when attached to a verb:

| | |
|---|---|
| Did you hear me on the radio (lit. 'in the radio')? | هَل سَمِعتَني في الراديو؟<br>hal samiعtanī fī r-rādyū? |

### *Activity 5*

Change these sentences using attached pronouns, as in the example.

١ وَجَدنا القطّة تحت الكرسي. **وَجَدناها تحت الكرسي.**

٢ هل وجدتَ المفتاح؟ ______

٣ سوف أشرب فنجان شاي. ______

٤ غسلَت فاطمة الزجاجات. ______

٥ سَمِعتُ الخَبَر في الراديو. ______

٦ كلّ يوم يَحضُرونَ اجتماعاً. ______

٧ سمِعنا الأولاد في الشارع. ______

٨ سَنفتح الباب بَعدَ ساعة *(after an hour)*. ______

## Notes about verbs in spoken Arabic

In general everyday spoken Arabic drops the final short vowels and ن na on the end of verbs. This means that تشربين tashrabīna (you *fem.* drink) becomes tashrabī, and يشربون yashrabūna (they drink) becomes yashrabū. In the past tense فتح fataḥa (he opened) becomes fataḥ; فتحتُ fataḥtu (I opened) and فتحتَ fataḥta (you, *masc.* opened) both become fataḥt. However, فتحتِ fataḥti (you *fem.* opened) does retain the -i ending.

The masculine plural is generally employed for all plural or dual subjects in spoken Arabic, meaning the feminine plural and dual verbs are only really a feature of Standard Arabic.

### In summary

- المُضارع al-muḍāriɛ (the *imperfect*) is used to describe both present and future events.
- The imperfect of basic verbs is formed with different prefixes and endings around a three-consonant stem, e.g. يَفتَح yaftaḥ (he opens), أفتَح aftaḥ (I open), يَفتحون yaftaḥūna (they open).
- The future indicators سَ sa- or سوف sawfa are often added before an imperfect verb when describing future events: سأذهب sa-ashrab (I'll drink), سوف نخرج sawfa nakhruj (we'll go out)..
- Attached pronouns can be added to verbs as well as nouns, e.g. سَمِعناهم samiɛnā*hum* (we heard *them*).

# 16 Irregular verbs

Most irregularities in Arabic verbs occur when one of the three root consonants of the verb is either و wāw or ي yā. These two letters are considered 'weak', effectively meaning they can change into vowels in certain word patterns and sometimes drop out altogether.

Other irregularities come about when a verb is 'doubled', having the same second and third root letter, or has hamza ( ء ) as one of the root consonants.

## Weak verbs

Weak verbs fall into three categories:
- و wāw or ي yā as first root letter (*assimilated* verbs)
- و wāw or ي yā as middle root letter (*hollow* verbs)
- و wāw or ي yā as final root letter (*defective* verbs)

### Assimilated verbs

Most assimilated verbs in common circulation have و wāw rather than ي yā as the first root letter. These verbs are relatively simple to remember and are irregular only in the imperfect tense, where the و wāw drops out altogether:

*(he finds)* yajid يَجِد ← *(he found)* wajada وَجَدَ

*(we arrive)* naṣil نَصِل ← *(we arrived)* waṣalnā وَصَلْنا

*(they describe)* yaṣifūna يَصِفونَ ← *(they described)* waṣafū وَصَفوا

*(she weighs)* tazin تَزِن ← *(she weighed)* wazanat وَزَنَت

## Activity 1

Change these past tense sentences to refer to everyday activities, as in the example:

١ وجدنا قِطّة في الشارع. **كُلّ يوم نَجِد قِطّة في الشارِع.**

٢ وَصَلتُ إلى المكتب صباحاً. ..............................

٣ وَصَفَت نادية رِحلتها *(her trip)* إلى باريس. ..............................

٤ وَجَدوا المِفتاح على المائدة. ..............................

٥ وَزَن الخبّاز العَجين *(the dough)*. ..............................

٦ وَصَلَ إلى وسط المدينة بالقِطار. ..............................

## Hollow verbs

Hollow verbs have و wāw or ي yā as the *second* root letter. They are called 'hollow' because the و wāw or ي yā in the middle often changes into a vowel. This can be a long vowel (ā, ū, ī) or a short vowel (a, u, i). This category includes some common verbs.

There are two main types of hollow verb, depending on the middle root letter, and these are shown below. The less common feminine plurals are shown in grey. Leave these until after you are familiar with the rest of the parts of the verb.

**Hollow verbs with و** wāw: **قال/يقول** *(to say)*

| *imperfect* | *past* | |
|---|---|---|
| aqūl أقول | qultu قُلتُ | أنا I |
| taqūl تَقول | qulta قُلتَ | you *(m.)* أنتَ |
| taqūlīna تَقولينَ | qulti قُلتِ | you *(f.)* أنتِ |
| yaqūl يَقول | qāla قالَ | he/it هو |
| taqūl تَقول | qālat قالَت | she/it هي |
| naqūl نَقول | qulnā قُلنا | we نَحنُ |
| taqūlūna تَقولونَ | qultum قُلتُم | you *(m. pl.)* أنتُم |
| taqulna تَقُلنَ | qultunna قُلتُنَّ | you *(f. pl.)* أنتُنَّ |
| yaqūlūna يَقولونَ | qālū قالوا | they *(m.)* هُم |
| yaqulna يَقُلنَ | qultna قُلنَ | they *(f.)* هُنَّ |

**Hollow verbs with ي yā: طار/يطير** *(to fly)*

| | *past* | *imperfect* |
|---|---|---|
| I أنا | ṭirtu طِرتُ | aṭīr أطير |
| you *(m.)* أنتَ | ṭirta طِرتَ | taṭīr تَطير |
| you *(f.)* أنتِ | ṭirti طِرتِ | taṭīrīna تَطيرينَ |
| he/it هو | ṭāra طارَ | yaṭīr يَطير |
| she/it هي | ṭārat طارَت | taṭīr تَطير |
| we نَحنُ | ṭirnā طِرنا | naṭīr نَطير |
| you *(m. pl.)* أنتُم | ṭirtum طِرتُم | taṭīrūna تَطيرونَ |
| you *(f. pl.)* أنتُنَّ | ṭirtunna طِرتُنَّ | taṭirna تطِرنَ |
| they *(m.)* هُم | ṭārū طاروا | yaṭīrūna يَطيرونَ |
| they *(f.)* هُنَّ | ṭirna طِرنَ | yaṭirna يطِرنَ |

With a few exceptions, hollow verbs fit into one of the two patterns shown above. Note:

- the past verb for هو, هي and هم has a long ā in the middle for *both* types of hollow verb
- the other past verbs have u or i in the middle
- the imperfect verb is characterised by a long ū for verbs with و wāw as middle root letter and a long ī for those with ي yā as middle root letter.

| | |
|---|---|
| We will fly to London next week. | سَنطير إلى لُندُن الأسبوع القادِم.<br>sa-naṭīr ilā lundun al-usbūع al-qādim. |
| I said to my husband 'Let's go'. | قُلتُ لِزوجي «هيا بنا!»<br>qultu l-zawjī 'hayā binā!' |
| He sold his ticket to Zaynab. | باعَ تَذكِرته لِزينَب.<br>bāعa tadhkiratuh li-zaynab. |
| They return from school by bus. | يعودونَ من المدرسة بالباص.<br>yaعūdūna min al-madrasa bil-bāṣ. |

### Activity 2

Choose one of the hollow verbs in the box to fill the gap in each sentence. Make sure you change the verb to match the subject. Note these time phrases which will show which tense you should be using:

yesterday ams أمس

tomorrow ghadan غَداً

every day kull yawm كُلّ يوم

next year as-sana al-qādima السنة القادمة

last month ash-shahr al-māḍī الشَهر الماضي

| | | |
|---|---|---|
| طار/يَطير *(to fly)* | عاد/يَعود *(to return)* | زار/يَزور *(to visit)* |
| قال/يَقول *(to say)* | باع/يَبيع *(to sell)* | فاز/يَفوز *(to win)* |

١ (أنا) **عُدتُ** من القاهرة أمس.

٢ (نَحنُ) سَـ________ أُمّنا في المُستَشفى غداً.

٣ هل (أنتِ) ________ تذكرتك على الانترنَت أمس؟

٤ كُلّ يوم (هم) ________ التُفّاح *(apples)* في السوق.

٥ أمس (هِيَ) ________ «سأزوركُم غداً.».

٦ (هُوَ) ________ سيّارته لصديقه الشهر الماضي.

٧ كُلّ يوم ________ الطائرة فوق بيتنا.

٨ ________ دينا بِكَأس التنس *(tennis cup)* في الشهر الماضي.

An important hollow verb is كان/يكون kān/yakūn (to be). Although many statements in the present don't include the verb 'to be', it is needed in the past and the future:

| | |
|---|---|
| I am in the bank today. | أنا في البنك اليوم.<br>anā fī l-bank al-yawm. |
| I was in the museum yesterday. | كُنتُ في المَتحَف أمس.<br>kuntu fī l-matḥaf ams. |
| I'll be in the office tomorrow. | سَأكون في المكتَب غداً.<br>sa-akūn fī l-maktab ghadan. |

The present tense of the verb 'to be' *is* used following لِـ li- (in order to), أن an (that), and other similar words:

| | |
|---|---|
| We went to the party in order to be with our friends. | ذَهَبنا إلى الحفلة لِنكون مَعَ أصحابنا.<br>dhahabnā ilā al-ḥafla li-nakūn maعa aṣḥābnā. |
| The fish has to be fresh. ('It is necessary that the fish is fresh.') | يَجِب أن يكون السَمَك طازجاً.*<br>yajib an yakūn as-samak ṭāzijan. |

* the extra alif is added after the verb يكون yakūn (see Case Notes Unit 14)

## *Activity 3*

Change these sentences to refer to the past, as in the example.

١ أنا في المَصنَع. ← **كُنتُ في المَصنَع.** ..................

٢ نَحنُ في المدرسة. ← ..................

٣ أختي مُقيمة *(resident)* في السَعودية. ← ..................

٤ هم في المدرسة. ← ..................

٥ هل أنتِ في بيتِك؟ ← ..................

Now write them again in the future, e.g.:

١ **سَأكون في المَصنَع.**

## Activity 4

Read this passage where Hajj Khayri (الحاجّ خيري al-ḥājj khayrī) is telling his grandchildren (أحفاد aḥfād) why he thinks the internet has made life easier. (ḥājj is a term of respect for someone who has been on the pilgrimage to Mecca.)

قال الحاجّ خيري لأحفاده...

«شبكة الانترنت هي سوق لِمَن يشتري *(buys)* أو يبيع أيّ شيء وكُلّ شيء. مُنذُ سَنَوات، ذَهَبتُ لِشِراء *(to buy)* تذكِرة أطير بها إلى لَندَن لأزور أخي شلبي المُقيم هناك. كان مكتب شَركة الطَيران بعيداً في وسط المدينة. دَفَعنا *(we paid)* ثَمَن التذكرة ثم قالوا لنا: حِين *(when)* تعودون بعد ثلاثة أيّام سَتكون التذكرة مَوجودة.»

ضَحِكَ *(laughed)* الأولاد وهم يقولون «ها! ها! ثلاثة أيام لشراء تذكرة!»

1 Where did Hajj Khayri want to travel a few years ago?
2 Who did he want to visit there?
3 Where did he have to go to buy the ticket?
4 How long did they tell him he would have to wait before his ticket was available?
5 Why do you think the children find this funny?

Now underline all the examples of *hollow* verbs you can find in the passage.

## Defective verbs

Defective verbs have و wāw or ي yā as the *final* root letter. There are several different types, but the most common feature is a long vowel in place of the third root letter. Here are some examples:

جرَى/يجري jarā/yajrī (to run)

دعا/يدعو daعā/yadعū (to invite)

مشَى/يمَشي mashā/yamshī (to walk)

نسِي/ينَسى nasiya/yansā (to forget)

رمى/يرمي ramā/yarmī (to throw)

شكا/يشكو shakā/yashkū (to complain)

The detailed rules for how to spell and form defective verbs are somewhat complicated and need to be learnt individually by consulting a comprehensive Arabic grammar or verb reference. However, as a rule of thumb the imperfect is largely consistent, whereas the the final long ā vowel in the past will often turn into aw or ay before an ending which begins with a consonant:

(we complained) shakawnā شكَونا ← (he complained) shakā شكا

(I threw) ramaytu رَمَيتُ ← (he threw) ramā رَمَى

(you *pl.* walked) mashaytum مَشَيتُم ← (he walked) mashā مَشى

## Other irregular verbs

Other irregularities arise from:

- the second and third root consonants being the same letter (*doubled* verbs)
- one of the roots being hamza (ء)

### *Doubled verbs*

Doubled verbs sometimes combine the second and third root letters with a shadda (ـّ), e.g. رَدّ radda (he answered), and sometimes separate them, e.g. رَدَدتُ radadtu (I answered). The rule determining this is:

- third root letter followed directly by vowel (long or short) = combined
- third root letter *not* followed directly by vowel = separate

If you take any part of the present/future or past verb tenses and apply the rule above, you can work out how to form the appropriate double verb. For example:

| *result* | *subject* | *tense* | *root* |
|---|---|---|---|
| radadnā رَدَدنا | نحن | الماضي | ر / د / د *(answer)* |
| dallat دَلَّت | هي | الماضي | د / ل / ل *(show/prove)* |
| yaẓunn(u*) يَظُنّ | هو | المضارع | ظ / ن / ن *(think)* |
| tashukkūna تشُكّون | أنتم | المضارع | ش / ك / ك *(doubt)* |

* For the purposes of deciding whether or not to write the doubled root together, any final u in the imperfect المضارع is taken into account (see Unit 15)

The result of applying this rule is:

- doubled verbs in the imperfect المضارع are almost always written with a shadda (ـّ)
- doubled verbs in the past الماضي are written with a shadda for هو, هي and هم but with separate letters for the other subjects

## Activity 5

Complete this chart of doubled verbs, as in the example.

| *result* | *subject* | *tense* | *root* |
|---|---|---|---|
| (radadtu) رَدَدتُ | أنا | الماضي | ر / د / د *(answer)* |
| .................... | أنا | المضارع | ش / ك / ك *(doubt)* |
| .................... | أنتِ | المضارع | د / ل / ل *(show/prove)* |
| .................... | نحن | المضارع | ظ / ن / ن *(think)* |

| | | | |
|---|---|---|---|
| ع / د / د *(count)* | الماضي | أنا | ________ |
| م / د / د *(stretch)* | الماضي | هي | ________ |
| ض / م / م *(join)* | الماضي | هم | ________ |

## *Activity 6*

Now use six of the verbs you formed in Activity 5 to fill the gaps in this picture story about an air hostess (مُضيفة muḍīfa) and her passengers (رُكّاب rukkāb), as in the example. Don't worry about understanding every word, just try to get the gist and work out which verb might fit in the gap.

١ مَدّت المُضيفة يَدها وقالت «تَفَضَّل! سندوتش الدجاج.»

٢ أنا ________ عليها «آسِف. أنا طَلَبتُ *(I ordered)* سندوتش جبنة *(cheese)* أنا نَباتي *(vegetarian)*!»

٣ «لا. أنا ________ النباتيين وهم ثلاثة وأنت لستُ مِنهم. تَفَضَّل سندوتش الدجاج!»

٤ «يا آنِسة. أنا لا ________ في ذاكِرتي *(my memory)*. أنا نَباتي، لا آكل اللَّحم!»

٥ قال راكِب «ما كلّ هذا؟ كُنّا ________ أنك رجل عاقِل! لِماذا لا تأكل الدجاج يا أخي؟»

٦ وَقَفَ الرُكّاب و ________ أصواتهم *(their voices)* إليه وقالوا «الدجاج مُفيد لك! كُلّنا نأكل الدجاج!»

## Verbs with hamza as root letter

It is possible for verbs to have hamza (ء) as one of the root letters. These verbs are not strictly speaking irregular, but there are some aspects which need clarification:

1 When a verb has hamza as the *first* root letter, e.g. أَخَذَ/يَأْخُذ a'khadha/ya'khudh (to take), the أنا āna part of the imperfect is written with a special madda sign above the alif (آ). This is pronounced as long ā:

*(I take)* ākhudh آخُذ = أخُذ + أ

*(I eat)* ākul آكُل = أكُل + أ

2 The hamza may be written in a number of different ways:

- on an alif: أ , e.g. يأخُذ ya'khudh (he takes)
- on a wāw: ؤ , e.g. نَبطؤ nabṭu' (we slow down)
- on a yā with no dots: ئ/ئـ , e.g. سَئِمَ sa'ima (he loathed)

You will begin to get a feel for how to spell hamza as you become more familiar with individual examples.

## Very irregular verbs

There are a few verbs which display more than one irregular feature (e.g. weak *and* have hamza as a root letter), and these can behave unpredictably. Common examples are the verbs 'to see': رأى/يَرى ra'ā/yarā, and 'to come': جاء/يجيء jā'a/yajī'.

| | |
|---|---|
| Do you *(m.)* want to see the pyramids? | هل تريد أن ترى الأهرام؟<br>hal turīd an tarā al-ahrām? |
| Where did she see the mouse? | أين رَأت الفأر؟<br>ayna ra'at al-fa'r? |
| We come here every day. | نجيء هنا كلّ يوم.<br>najī' hunā kull yawm. |
| I came yesterday but I didn't find anyone. | جِئتُ أمس ولكنّي لم أجِد أحداً.<br>ji'tu ams wa-lākinnī lam ajid aḥadan. |

## *Activity 7*

With the help of the glossary read this passage about what Bashir (بَشير) does every day. Decide if the sentences below are true or false. Remember to read for gist and not worry about understanding every word.

1 Bashir is Lebanese.
2 He's a football coach.
3 In the past he was an accountant in a bank.
4 Every morning he drinks a cup of coffee ...
5 ... and eats a sandwich.
6 He takes the bus to the tennis club.
7 He only teaches tennis to girls.
8 He teaches them how to hold their rackets.
9 In the evening he sometimes visits his mother.
10 Sometimes he plays chess with his friends.

بشير مُدَرِّب التَنِس في النادي، وهو من بيروت في لُبنان. في الماضي كان مهندساً في مصنع ولكنّه الآن يرى أن حياة المدرّب أفضَل.
صباح كلّ يوم، يَشرَب بشير فنجان شاي، ويأكُل سَندَويتش جُبنة ثم يَأخذ الباص إلى نادي التنس.
بشير يَصِف للأولاد والبنات كيف يمسكون المضارب ويردّون الكرة فوق الشبكة، ويقول «عينك على الكرة دائماً!».
في المساء يعود بشير إلى بيته وأحياناً يزور أخته أو يلعب الشَطرَنج مع أصحابه.

| | |
|---|---|
| *coach* = mudarrib مُدَرِّب | *life* = ḥiyā حياة |
| *to hold* = yamsik يَمسِك | *rackets* = maḍārib مَضارِب |
| *better* = afḍal أفضَل | *ball* = kura كُرة |
| *sometimes* = aḥyānan أحياناً | *chess* = ash-shaṭaranj الشَطرَنج |

Now imagine you are Bashir and change the passage to أنا anā. Begin like this:

**أنا مُدَرّب التَنِس في النادي...**

## In summary

- Irregularities in Arabic verbs usually stem from one of the three root consonants being و wāw or ي yā ('weak' letters).

- Assimilated verbs have a weak *first* root (almost always و wāw) and are mainly regular, except that the initial و wāw drops out in the imperfect: وصل/يصل waṣala/yaṣil (to arrive).

- Hollow verbs have a weak *second* root and are characterised by a long or short vowel in the middle, e.g. قال/يقول qāla/yaqūl (to say); طار/يطير ṭāra/yaṭīr (to fly).

- Defective verbs have a weak *third* root and are characterised by a long vowel or dipthong (ay or aw) in place of the third root consonant, e.g. مشى/يمشي mashā/yamshī (to walk).

- Other irregularities are caused by a doubled second and third root letter, e.g. ردّ/يردّ radda/yarudd (to answer), or by hamza (ء) being one of the root letters, e.g. أكل/يأكل 'akala/ya'kul (to answer).

unit 17

# Forms of the verb

## Introduction

The Arabic root system shows itself most clearly through the forms of the verb. By adding additional letters before and between the three root letters different, but related, meanings are created. For example, دَرَسَ darasa means 'he learnt', but when the middle root letter is doubled to create دَرَّسَ darrasa the meaning changes to 'he taught'. In a similar way كَتَبوا katabū means 'they wrote'; the addition of an alif after the first root letter produces كاتَبوا kātabū 'they corresponded with'; the further addition of ta in front of the first root produces تكاتبوا takātabū 'they corresponded with each other'.

The derived forms are referred to by Arabists as Form II, Form III, etc. (Form I being the basic verb form). Native speakers will usually refer to them in the المضارع *(imperfect)* form using the root فعل (to do).

There are nine derived forms altogether in modern Arabic (II–X), but Form IX is rare. Each form has a past and imperfect pattern connected with it, for example the doubling of the middle root letter in دَرَّسَ darrasa is Form II, whereas the addition of an alif after the first root letter in كاتَبوا kātabū is Form III. It is important to realise that although the derived forms add letters before and between the root consonants, the prefixes and endings which show the subject of the verb remain the same as they are for the basic verbs: دَرَّسَ darrasa 'he taught'; درَّستُ darrastu 'I taught'; درَّسنا darrasnā 'we taught'; etc.

In theory every root could be put into all ten forms, but in practice an individual root will have only particular derived forms in common circulation. This unit will give you an overview of the forms and present some useful examples. Don't expect to master all the detail straight away. As you begin to feel more comfortable with the system of derived forms and their related meanings, you will find they are a helpful way of expanding your vocabulary.

The eight commonly used derived forms fall into three groups which share characteristics:

- Forms II, III and IV
- Forms V and VI
- Forms VII, VIII and X

Each derived form has meaning patterns connected to it. Although these meaning patterns will not always be obvious in individual derived verbs, they are a good general guide and can help you to guess at the meaning of unknown vocabulary.

## Forms II, III and IV

- Form II *doubles* the middle root letter
- Form III adds a long ā *after* the first root letter
- Form IV adds a short a (أ) *before* the first root letter in the past tense

Forms II, III and IV are all vowelled with fatḥas in the past tense and with the sequence ḍamma/(fatḥa)/kasra in the imperfect. This table shows the patterns using the root letters فعل:

| *example* | المضارع | الماضي | |
|---|---|---|---|
| *(to heat)* سَخَّنَ/يُسَخِّن | yufaɛɛil يُفَعِّل | faɛɛala فَعَّلَ | *II* |
| *(to travel)* سَافَرَ/يُسافِر | yufāɛil يُفاعِل | fāɛala فاعَلَ | *III* |
| *(to take out)* أخرَجَ/يُخرِج | yufɛil يُفعِل | afɛala أفعَلَ | *IV* |

- Form II is often used for actions carried out on someone/something else:

  يُجهِّز yujahhiz = 'to make something ready', or 'to prepare' (basic form = يَجهِز yajhiz 'to be ready')

  It can also intensify the meaning:

  يُكَسِّر yukassir = 'to break something into pieces', or 'to smash' (basic form = يكسِر yaksir 'to break')

- Form III can carry the meaning of *trying* to perform an action:
  يُسابِق yusābiq = 'to try to be in front', or 'to race against'
  (basic form = يَسبِق yasbiq 'to be in front/to precede')
  Or of doing something with somone else:
  يُحادِث yuḥādith = 'to talk to someone', or 'to converse with'
- Form IV, like Form II, is used for actions carried out on someone/something else,
  يُجلِس yujlis = 'to cause someone to sit down', or 'to seat'
  (basic form = يَجلِس yajlis 'to sit down')

| | |
|---|---|
| We heat the bread in the oven. | نُسَخِّن الخُبز في الفُرن.<br>nusakhkhin al-khubz fī l-furn. |
| They travelled to Jordan by boat. | سافَروا إلى الأُردُنّ بالمَركِب.<br>sāfarū ilā l-urdunn bil-markib. |
| The girl took out the trash. | أخرَجَت البِنت الزُبالة.<br>akhrajat al-bint az-zubāla. |

Note that the vowelling of derived forms does *not* vary as it does with basic verbs. For example, a Form II verb in the imperfect will always be vowelled يُفَعِّل yufaعّil, and a Form IV verb in the past tense will always be vowelled أفعَل afعala.

## Activity 1

Look at these derived verbs and decide if they are Form II, III or IV, as in the example.

| | | |
|---|---|---|
| *Form II* | naẓẓafa نَظَّف / yunaẓẓif يُنَظِّف | to clean |
| ________ | ajlasa أجلَس / yujlis يُجلِس | to seat |
| ________ | ḥādatha حادَث / yuḥādith يُحادِث | to converse with |
| ________ | jahhaza جَهَّز / yujahhiz يُجهِّز | to prepare |
| ________ | ḥāwala حاوَل / yuḥāwil يُحاوِل | to try |
| ________ | akhbara أخبَر / yukhbir يُخبِر | to inform |
| ________ | sallaḥa صَلَّح / yuṣalliḥ يَصلِّح | to repair |
| ________ | sābaqa سابَق / yusābiq يُسابِق | to race |
| ________ | kassara كَسَّر / yukassir يُكَسِّر | to smash |

## Activity 2

Match the Arabic sentences to the English, trying to guess at the meaning of the verbs from words you already know with the same root letters.

| | |
|---|---|
| *a) Bashir coaches the children in the club.* | ١ هل تُصوِّر الحَيَوانات؟ |
| *b) We feed the birds.* | ٢ يُسافِرونَ إلى فَرَنسا بالطائرة. |
| *c) They travel to France by airplane.* | ٣ يُدَرِّب بشير الأولاد في النادي. |
| *d) I treat guests as my friends.* | ٤ تُحضِر الممَرِّضة الدواء. |
| *e) Do you photograph animals?* | ٥ أعامل الضُيوف كَأصحابي. |
| *f) The nurse brings the medicine.* | ٦ نُؤَكِّل الطُيور. |

## Activity 3

Put the sentences in Activity 2 into the past, for example:

hal sawwarta l-ḥayawānāt? ١ هل صَوَّرتَ الحَيَوانات؟
*(Did you [m.] photograph animals?)*

## Forms V and VI

| | الماضي | المضارع | example |
|---|---|---|---|
| *V* | تَفَعَّل tafaععala | يَتَفَعَّل yatafaععal | تَحَدَّث/يَتَحَدَّث *(to speak)* |
| *VI* | تَفاعَل tafāعala | يَتَفاعَل yatafāعal | تَعاوَن/يَتَعاوَن *(to cooperate)* |

Forms V and VI both add ta (تَـ) before the first root letter. In the *past* tense, Form V = ta (تَـ) + Form II; Form VI = ta (تَـ) + Form III. In the *imperfect* tense, Forms V and VI are vowelled throughout with fatḥas (a).

- Form VI often carries the meaning of doing something together as a group:
  yataعāwan يَتَعاوَن = 'to help each other', or 'to cooperate' (root: عَوَن = help/aid)
- Form V tends to be intransitive (i.e. actions *not* carried out on something/someone else).

| | |
|---|---|
| Do you speak Arabic? | هل تَتَحَدَّث العَرَبيّة؟<br>hal tataḥaddath al-ع arabiyya? |
| The ministers met for two days and cooperated on the peace plan. | تقابَلَ الوزراء لِمُدّة يومين وتعاونوا في خِطّة السَلام.<br>taqābala l-wuzarā' li-muddat yawmayn wa-taعāwanū fī khiṭṭat is-salām. |

## *Activity 4*

Read this story about Mr Jones (السَيِّد جونز) and underline all the Form V and VI verbs you can see.

السَيِّد جونز من ويلز ويُحاول أن يَتَعَلَّم العَرَبية. مُستَواه *(his level)* يَتَقَدَّم مع كلّ دَرس لأنّه *(because he)* يحاول أن

يتذكّر الكَلمات العَرَبية. حين يَتَقابَل الناس في الشارع صباحاً، يَتَبادَلون التَحيّة *(greetings)* والسلام ويقولون: «صباح الخير!» سَألَ السَيِّد جونز المدرّس عن الرَدّ المُناسِب *(appropriate)*، وتَدَرَّبَ على قول «صباح النور!» لِمُدة يَومَين.

Now try to guess the meaning of the verbs you underlined from the context. Write the verbs in the present and past next to the English below, as in the example.

| | | |
|---|---|---|
| learn **تعَلَّم/يَتَعَلَّم** | meet up ________ | practise ________ |
| remember ________ | progress ________ | exchange ________ |

### Activity 5

Change these sentences according to the subject in brackets, as in the example.

١ يُحاول أن يتعلّم العربيّة. (هي)

**تحاول أن تتعلّم العربيّة.**

٢ تذكّر السيّد جونز الكلمات العربيّة. (أنا)

٣ حين يتقابل الناس، يتبادلون التحيّة. (نحن)

٤ يقولون: «صباح الخير.» (أنتِ)

٥ سأل عن الردّ المناسب. (هم)

٦ تدرّب على قول «صباح النور». (أنتَ)

## Forms VII, VIII and X

| | الماضي | المضارع | example |
|---|---|---|---|
| *VII* | اِنفَعَلَ infaعala | يَنفَعِل yanfaعil | اِنكَسَرَ/يَنكَسِر *(to be broken)* |
| *VIII* | اِفتَعَلَ iftaعala | يَفتَعِل yaftaعil | اِجتَمَعَ/يَجتَمِع *(to meet)* |
| *X* | اِستفعَلَ istafعala | يَستفعِل yastafعil | اِستَعلَمَ/يَستَعلِم *(to enquire)* |

Forms VII, VIII and X all start with i (اِ) in the past tense and are all vowelled with two fatḥas (a) and a kasra (i) in the imperfect. Form VII also adds n (نْ) *before* the first root letter; Form VIII adds ta (تَـ) *after* the first root letter; and Form X adds sta (ستَـ) *before* the first root letter.

- Form VII is often passive:

  انكسر/ينكسر inkasara/yankasir = 'to be broken'

  (كسر/يكسر kasara/yaksir = to break)

- Form VIII is a common verbal form. However, the meaning patterns are more diverse and difficult to pin down. It can have a reflexive meaning (performing an action on oneself):

  اجتمع/يجتمع ijtamaɛa/yajtamiɛ = 'to collect yourselves' or 'to meet up' (جمع/يجمع jamaɛa/yajmaɛ = to collect)

  اشتغل/يشتغل ishtaghala/yashtaghil = 'to occupy yourself' or 'to work' (شغل shughl = occupation/work)

- Form X can mean to consider something to have an attribute. For example:

  استحسن/يستحسن istaḥsana/yastaḥsin = 'to consider good', or 'admire' (حَسَن ḥasan = good)

  or to ask for something:

  استعلم/يستعلم istaɛlama/yastaɛlim = 'to ask for information', or 'enquire' (علم ɛilm = knowledge)

Don't forget that the meaning patterns are for general guidance. Some derived verbs have no obvious connection with these patterns.

## Activity 6

Fill in the missing entries in this table, as in the example:

| Form | Present/future | Past | Meaning |
|------|----------------|------|---------|
| VIII | يَقتَرِب yaqtarib | اِقتَرَبَ iqtaraba | to approach |
| X | يَستَمتِع yastamtiɛ | | to enjoy |
| VII | | اِنقَلَبَ inqalaba | to be overturned |
| | يَستَمِع yastamiɛ | اِستَمَعَ istamaɛa | to listen |
| | يَستَحسِن yastaḥsin | | to admire |
| | | اِبتَكَرَ ibtakara | to create |
| | | اِستَخدَمَ istakhdama | to use |

## Activity 7

Look at these example sentences:

| | |
|---|---|
| They listened to the news on the radio. | استمعوا إلى الأخبار في الراديو.<br>istamaعū ilā l-akhbār fī r-rādyū. |
| We use the internet in our office. | نستخدم شَبَكة الانترنت في مكتبنا.<br>nastkhdim shabakat al-intarnat fī maktabnā. |
| The car approached the main street. | اقتربت السيّارة من الشارع الرَئيسي.<br>iqtariba s-sayyāra min ash-shāriع ar-ra'īsī. |
| Did you enjoy the party? | هل استمتعتَ بالحفلة؟<br>hal istamtaعta bil-ḥafla? |

Now decide how you would say these in Arabic:

1 Do you *(masc.)* use the internet in your office?
2 They use the internet in their office.
3 The bus approached the main street.
4 We approached our house.
5 I listen to the news on the radio.
6 Did you *(pl.)* enjoy the film (الفيلم)?

## Irregular verbs in derived forms

Weak and doubled verbs have varying features in the derived forms, depending on the particular root and form.

It is not possible to list all the variations here. However, there is some general guidance which will help you to recognise irregular verbs in the derived forms:

- Hollow and doubled verbs are regular in Forms II, III, V and VI. The weak middle root و wāw or ي yā' in hollow verbs does not change into a vowel and the second and third root letters of doubled verbs remain separate:

  حاوَل/يُحاوِل ḥāwala/yuḥāwil (to try); Form III: root ḥ/w/l حول

  رَدَّد/يُرَدِّد raddada/yuraddid (to repeat); Form II: root r/d/d ردد

تَنَاوَل/يَتَنَاوَل yatanāwal/tanāwal (to deal with); Form VI: root n/w/l نول

- Hollow and doubled verbs are irregular in Forms IV, VII, VIII and X. The irregularities are similar to the basic verb form, with hollow verbs replacing the second root letter with a long or short vowel and doubled verbs often combining the second and third root letters:

  أحَبَّ/يُحِبّ aḥabb/yuḥibb (to like); Form IV: root ḥ/b/b حبب

  اِستَرَاحَ/يَستَرِيح istarāḥa/yastarīḥ (to rest); Form X: root r/w/ḥ روح

- Defective verbs with و wāw or ي yā' as the final root letter are irregular in *all* the forms, ending in the characteristic long vowel: ī if the vowel preceding the third root letter in the regular pattern is kasra and ā if the vowel preceding it is fatḥa:

  اِشتَرَى/يَشتَري ishtarā/yashtarī (to buy); Form VIII: root sh/r/y شري

  أعطَى/يُعطي aʿṭā/yuʿṭī (to give); Form IV from root ع/ṭ/y عطي

## In summary

- Arabic features derived forms of the verb which modify the meaning of the root.
- There are eight derived forms in common use. They are produced by placing additional letters before and between the root letters.
- Forms II and III share characteristics, as do Forms V and VI, and Forms VII, VIII and X.
- An individual root will have particular derived forms in common circulation.

unit 18

# Making verbs negative

## Imperfect tense negative

The imperfect tense المضارع used for present and future statements is made negative by adding لا lā in front of the verb:

*(he doesn't take)* lā ya'khudh لا يأخُذ ← *(he takes)* ya'khudh يأخُذ

*(we don't travel)* lā nusāfir لا نُسافر ← *(we travel)* nusāfir نُسافر

*(I don't like)* lā uḥibb لا أحِبّ ← *(I like)* uḥibb أحِبّ

| | |
|---|---|
| I don't like ice-cream. | لا أحِبّ الآيس كريم.<br>lā uḥibb al-ays krīm. |
| The cook doesn't prepare salad. | لا يُجَهِّز الطَبّاخ السلَطة.<br>lā yajahhiz aṭ-ṭabākhkh as-salaṭa. |
| They don't live in tents. | لا يَسكُنونَ في خيام.<br>lā yaskunūna fī khiyām. |

## *Activity 1*

Make these sentences negative, as in the example.

١ تأخُذ فاطمة الأوتوبيس إلى المدرسة.

**لا تأخُذ فاطمة الأوتوبيس إلى المدرسة.**

٢ يغسل أحمد وجهه صباحاً.

..........................................

٣ أتحدّث العَرَبيّة. ..........................................

٤ تُسخِّنينَ الخبز في الفرن.

________________________________________

٥ يَجلس الأولاد في الفَصل ويَدرسونَ اللغة العربيّة.

________________________________________

٦ نَسكُن في وَسَط المدينة.

________________________________________

## *Activity 2*

Complete these sentences using the picture prompts, as in the example:

 ✔ أحِبّ القِطَط ولكنّي ... *(I like cats but …).*

 ✘ **لا أحبّ الكلاب.** *(I don't like dogs).*

١  ✔ أشرب قهوة ولكنّي...

 ✘ ________________________________________

٢  ✔ نُسافر بالمَركِب ولكنّنا...

 ✘ ________________________________________

٣ ABC ✔ تَدرس مُنى الاِنجِليزيّة ولكنّها...

أ ب ت ✘ ________________________________________

٤  ✔ يَستَمتِع يوسَف بالموسيقى ولكنّه...

 ✘ ________________________________________

٥  ✔ يبيعون السيّارات ولكنّهُم...

 ✘ ________________________________________

## Past tense negative

The past tense الماضي can be made negative in two ways:

ما + *past* verb: ما شَرِبتُ mā sharibtu (I didn't drink)

لَم + *present* verb: لَم أشرَب lam ashrab (I didn't drink)

لَم is more common in Modern Standard Arabic.

When the present verb follows لَم the parts of the verb ending in ن (أنتِ, أنتُم and هم) lose the final ن:

you *(fem.)* didn't drink = لَم تَشربي lam tashrabī

they didn't go = لَم يذهبوا* lam yadh-habū

you *(pl.)* didn't meet up = لَم تَتَقابَلوا* lam tataqābalū

* The silent alif is a spelling convention and is not pronounced.

| | |
|---|---|
| We didn't go to the party yesterday. | لم نذهب إلى الحفلة أمس.<br>lam nadh-hab ilā l-ḥafla ams. |
| The journey didn't last more than half an hour. | لم تَستَغرِق الرِحلة أكثَر من نِصف ساعة.<br>lam tastaghriq ar-riḥla akthar min niṣf sāɛa. |
| They travelled to the Red Sea, but they didn't listen to the weather forecast. | سافروا إلى البَحر الأحمر ولكنّهم لم يستَمِعوا إلى النَشرة الجَوِيّة.<br>sāfarū ilā l-baḥr al-aḥmar wa-lākinnahum lam yastamiɛū ilā l-nashra al-jawwiyya. |

## Activity 3

Fill the gaps with the correct form of the past verb in brackets, as in the example:

١ في الأسبوع الماضي أنا **ذَهَبتُ** (ذهب) إلى الحفلة ولكنّي

لم ________ (قابل) صديقي هناك.

٢ أمس ________ (ذهب) نورا إلى السوق ولكنّها لم

________ (وجد) الصابون *(soap)*.

٣ أنتَ لم ________ (كتب) رِسالة لأُختك في أمريكا.

٤ في الصيف الماضي نحن ________ (سافر) إلى اليابان *(Japan)*

ولكنّنا لم ________ (استمتع) بالرحلة.

٥ السنة الماضية ________ (اشترى) محمود سيّارة جديدة

ولكنّه لم ________ (استخدم) السيّارة فباعها.

٦ هم لم ________ (يستمع) إلى أمّهم و ________ (يكسر)

اللُعبة *(toy)*.

## Activity 4

Read the story about what happened to Mr Abbas (الأستاذ عَباس) on a journey last summer, and decide if these sentences are true or false.

1 Mr Abbas likes travelling by boat.
2 Last summer he went on a boat journey lasting two days.
3 He wasn't well prepared for the journey.
4 He booked a private cabin.
5 He didn't bring any seasickness medicine.
6 He listened to the weather forecast on the television.
7 He told the ship's doctor he wants to see a picture of a boat.

الأستاذ عباس يُحبّ أن يُسافر بالطائرة ولكنّه لا يحبّ البَحر. في الصيف الماضي لم يأخذ الطائرة وسافر بالمركب في رِحلة تَستَغرِق يَومين. كانت رِحلة عَذاب *(torture)* لأنّه لم يجهّز نفسه *(himself)* للسَفَر بالمركب أَبَداً...

لم يَحجِز قَمَرَة خاصّة.

لم يستمع إلى النشرة الجويّة في الراديو.

لم يُحضِر حُبوب *(pills)* دوار البحر.

ولم يلبس قُبَعته في الشمس.

قال الأستاذ عباس لِطَبيب المركب «أنا لا أستمتع بالمَراكِب يا دكتور. أنا لا أُريد أن أرى حتى صورة مَركِب في حَياتي بعد اليوم.»

## *Activity 5*

Now imagine you are Mr Abbas and retell the story. Start like this:

**أُحبّ أن أُسافر بالطائرة ولكنّي...**

## ليس 'not to be'

To make non-verbal sentences negative, there is a special verb ليس laysa, meaning 'not to be'. This unusual verb looks like the past tense, but has a present meaning:

(*I am not*) lastu لَستُ (أنا)

(*you* m. *are not*) lasta لَستَ (أنتَ)

(*you* f. *are not*) lasti لَستِ (أنتِ)

(*he/it is not*) laysa لَيسَ (هو)

(*she/it is not*) laysat لَيسَت (هي)

(*we are not*) lasnā لَسنا (نحن)

(*you* pl. *are not*) lastum لَستُم (أنتم)

(*they are not*) laysū ليسوا (هم)

| | | |
|---|---|---|
| He isn't in the house. | ليس في البيت. | laysa fī l-bayt. |
| I'm not Nadya. | لستُ نادية. | lastu nādiya. |
| She's not a nurse. | لَيسَت ممرّضة. | laysat mumarriḍa. |

### In summary

- The negative of a present verb is formed by adding لا in front of the verb: لا أعرف lā aɛrif (I don't know).
- The negative of the past tense is formed by either:
  – adding ما in front of the past verb:
  ما كتبتُ mā katabtu (I didn't write), or
  – adding لم in front of a present verb:
  لم أكتُب lam aktub (I didn't write)
  لم is more common in Modern Standard Arabic.
- There is a special verb ليس laysa, 'not to be', used to make non-verbal sentences negative.

unit 19

# Nouns and adjectives formed from verbs

By now you should be developing a feel for how root sequences are the foundation of Arabic, on which the richness of the language is built. You have seen these roots in action in the derived forms of the verb and the broken plurals. It is also possible to put the roots into other patterns to produce nouns and adjectives with associated meanings.

## Nouns of place

Many nouns describing places where particular things happen are formed using the مَفعَل mafعal pattern:

مَصنَع maṣnaع ('place of manufacture', i.e. factory), from the root صنع (manufacture/make)

مَكتَب maktab ('place of writing', i.e. office/study), from the root كتب (write)

مَدخَل madkhal ('place of entry', i.e. entrance), from the root دخل (enter)

In other words, by adding مَـ ma before the first root letter and fatḥa (a) after the second root letter, a noun of place is created associated with the particular root sequence.

There are some minor variations possible in the pattern. Occasionally, the second vowel is a kasra (i) as in مَجلِس majlis ('place of sitting', i.e. council), and sometimes the pattern ends in ة as in مَدرَسة madrasa ('place of study', i.e. school).

Whatever the singular variations, nouns of place share a common plural pattern: مَفاعِل mafāɛil.

| *singular* | *plural* |
|---|---|
| مَصنَع maṣnaɛ *factory* | مَصانِع maṣāniɛ *factories* |
| مَدرَسة madrasa *school* | مَدارِس madāris *schools* |

## *Activity 1*

Look at these nouns of place and complete the plural column:

| *singular* | *plural* | |
|---|---|---|
| مَجلِس majlis *council* | ______ | ١ |
| مَدخَل madkhal *entrance* | ______ | ٢ |
| مَكتَب maktab *office* | ______ | ٣ |
| مَخرَج makhraj *exit* | ______ | ٤ |
| مَعرَض maɛraḍ *exhibition* | ______ | ٥ |
| مَتحَف mathaf *museum* | ______ | ٦ |
| مَلعَب malɛab *playing field* | ______ | ٧ |
| مَسرَح masraḥ *theatre* | ______ | ٨ |

## Verbal nouns

English forms nouns from verbs by adding endings such as *-ment*, *-tion*, *-ing* and *-ance*:

employ → employment

educate → education

publish → publishing

perform → performance

Arabic uses different patterns to form verbal nouns depending on the type of verb.

## Verbal nouns: basic verbs

Nouns from basic verbs need to be learnt individually, although there are some common patterns. Look at these verbs and their related nouns:

| *Verbal noun* | *Verb (past/present)* | *Meaning* |
|---|---|---|
| dhahāb ذَهاب | ذهب/يذهب | to go |
| kitāba كِتابة | كتب/يكتب | to write |
| ؏awda عَودة | عاد/يعود | to return |
| khurūj خروج | خرج/يخرج | to go out |
| dukhūl دُخول | دخل/يدخل | to enter |
| shurb شُرب | شرب/يشرب | to drink |
| la؏ib لَعِب | لعب/يلعب | to play |
| ziyāra زِيارة | زار/يزور | to visit |
| ṭayr طَير | طار/يطير | to fly |
| radd رَدّ | رَدّ/يرُدّ | to answer |

You can see that فُعول fu؏ūl, فَعال fa؏āl and فَعل fa؏l are recurring patterns for verbal nouns. To find the noun from a particular basic verb, however, you will need to look it up in a dictionary.

Verbal nouns can be used to make general statements:

| | |
|---|---|
| Going out at night is dangerous here. | الخُروج في الليل خَطِر هنا.<br>al-khurūj fī l-layl khaṭir hunā. |
| Drinking water is good for your heath. | شُرب الماء مُفيد لِصِحّتك.<br>shurb al-mā' mufīd li-ṣiḥḥatak. |
| Entry forbidden! | مَمنوع الدُخول!<br>mamnū؏ ad-dukhūl |

If the verbal noun comes directly before another noun, as in شرب الماء shurb al-mā', it will not have the article الـ al as this is an إضافة iḍāfa construction (see Unit 10).

As well as being used for general concepts such as 'going' and 'entry', verbal nouns are widely used in Arabic in place of a second verb. For example, 'I want to go to the museum' can be expressed in Arabic as 'I want *that I go* to the museum' using أن (that), or a verbal noun can be used in place of the second verb:

urīd an adh-hab ilā l-matḥaf. أريد أن أذهب إلى المتحف.

urīd adh-dhahāb ilā l-matḥaf. أريد الذهاب إلى المتحف.

Likewise,

| | |
|---|---|
| Bashir likes to play tennis. | يُحِبّ بشير لَعِب التنس.<br>yuḥibb bashīr laعib at-tanis. |
| I went to the hospital to visit my uncle. | ذهبتُ إلى المُستَشفى لِزيارة خالي.<br>dhahbtu ilā l-mustashfā li-ziyārat khālī. |

## *Activity 2*

Rephrase these sentences using a verbal noun from the table on page 125, as in the example.

١ نُريد أن نزور المتحف. **نريد زيارة المتحف.**

٢ نُريد أن نذهب إلى البنك. ________

٣ أريد أن أكتب رِسالة *(message)* لأمّي. ________

٤ أحبّ أن أخرج من البيت. ________

٥ تُحبّ نادية أن تلعب مع أصحابها. ________

٦ يَجِب علينا أن نعود إلى المكتب. ________

## Verbal nouns: derived forms

Unlike basic verbs, the patterns for verbal nouns from the derived forms are predictable, with only Form III having an alternative. This table shows you the verbal nouns for the different forms. Some of the examples may already be familiar and these can help you to remember the patterns.

| *Example* | *Verbal noun* | *Verb* | *Form* |
|---|---|---|---|
| *preparation* tajhīz تَجهيز | tafعīl تَفعيل | فَعَّل/يُفَعِّل | II |
| *dispute* khilāf خِلاف | fiعāl فِعال | فاعَل/يُفاعِل | III |
| *conversation* muḥādatha مُحادثة | mufāعala مُفاعلة <u>or</u> | | |
| *information* iعlām إعلام | ifعāl إفعال | أفعَل/يُفعِل | IV |
| *progression* taqaddum تَقَدُّم | tafaععul تَفَعُّل | تفَعَّل/يتفعَّل | V |
| *cooperation* taعāwun تَعاوُن | tafāعul تَفاعُل | تَفاعَل/يَتَفاعَل | VI |
| *withdrawal* insiḥāb اِنسحاب | infiعāl اِنفعال | اِنفَعَل/يَنفَعِل | VII |
| *meeting* ijtimāع اِجتِماع | iftiعāl اِفتعال | اِفتَعَل/يَفتَعِل | VIII |
| *use/usage* istikhdām اِستِخدام | istifعāl اِستفعال | اِستَفعَل/يَستَفعِل | X |

Verbal nouns from the derived forms tend to form their plurals using the sound feminine plural ـات (-āt):

| | | |
|---|---|---|
| meetings | ijtimāعāt | اجتِماعات |
| preparations | tajhīzāt | تَجهيزات |

### *Activity 3*

Below is a passage written by a wife about her relationship with her husband. First look through the passage and see if you can find out how much the husband helps around the house. Try to get the general gist without worrying too much about understanding every word.

«حياتي كِفاح. زوجي صَحَفي في وِزارة الإعلام ورِسالته في الحياة هي النِضال ضد النِفاق والفساد.

خِلافنا الوحيد هو أنّه لا يجد الوَقت ليُساعِدني في تَجهيز الأكل، أو تدريس شَيء للأولاد، أو في تصليح هذا أو تنظيف تلك. كما أن تذكّر المُناسبات، ومُحادثة الأُسرة، وإرسال الزُهور كلّها مَسئوليّتي أنا وَحدي.»

Now read the translation below and fill in the missing words:

'My life is a struggle. My __________ is a journalist in the Ministry of __________ and his mission in __________ is the fight against hypocrisy and corruption.

Our one __________ is that he doesn't __________ the time to help me in __________ the food, or __________ anything to the children, or in __________ this or cleaning that. Just as __________ occasions, __________ to the family and sending flowers are all only my responsibility.'

Can you underline all the Arabic words in the passage that are verbal nouns?

### Activity 4

Choose a verbal noun from the box to fill each gap in the sentences below.

| | | | | | |
|---|---|---|---|---|---|
| الامتحان *(examination)* | الاستماع | اقتراب | الانقلاب *(uprising)* | الاجتماع | استقبال *(reception)* |

١ الوزير يريد __________ إلى خطّتنا.

٢ انسحبت جيوش *(armies)* الملك من المدينة بعد __________.

٣ حجزنا قاعة *(hall)* كبيرة لهذا __________ المهم.

٤ مَن سيكون في __________ الوَفد *(delegation)* الأمريكي في المَطار؟

٥ شعرت *(felt)* ليلى بالخوف مع __________ وقت __________.

## Active and passive participles

You can form active and passive participles from verbs. An active participle will show the 'doer', or subject, of the action; a passive participle will show the 'receiver', or object, of the action.

For basic verbs, active participles are formed using the pattern فاعِل fāعil:

| | | | | |
|---|---|---|---|---|
| لَعَبَ/يَلعَب | *to play* | ← | لاعِب lāعib | *player/(s.o./smth.) playing* |
| كَتَبَ/يكتُب | *to write* | ← | كاتِب kātib | *writer/(s.o./smth.) writing* |
| رَجَعَ/يَرجَع | *to return* | ← | راجِع rājiع | *returner/(s.o./smth.) returning* |

Passive participles are formed using the pattern مَفعول mafعūl:

| | |
|---|---|
| *(something) broken* maksūr مَكسور ← *to break* كَسَرَ/يَكسِر | |
| *(something) drunk* mashrūb مَشروب ← *to drink* شَرِبَ/يَشرَب | |
| *(something) washed* maghsūl مغسول ← *to wash* غَسَلَ/يَغسِل | |

These participles can be used as either nouns or adjectives, for example مكسور maksūr can mean 'broken' or 'a broken item'.

In the derived forms, active and passive participles are formed by taking the imperfect verb and:
- replacing the intitial يُـ yu- or يَـ ya- with مُـ mu-
- using a final kasra (i) for the active participle and a final fatḥa (a) for the passive participle

| | |
|---|---|
| *trainer* mudarrib مُدَرِّب ← *trains* yudarrib يُدرِّب | |
| *trained (person)* mudarrab مُدَرَّب | |
| *viewer* mushāhid مُشاهِد ← *views* yushāhid يُشاهد | |
| *viewed (item)* mushāhad مُشاهَد | |
| *capable (person)* mutamakkin مُتَمَكِّن ← *is able* yatamakkan يَتمَكّن | |
| *enabled (item)* mutamakkan مُتَمَكّن | |
| *user* mustakhdim مُستَخدِم ← *use* yastakhdim يستخدم | |
| *used (item)* mustakhdam مُستَخدَم | |

## Activity 5

اِختفى اللاعب المشهور ميمو سلطان تمّاماً!

The famous football player Mimo Sultan has completely disappeared!

What is happening tomorrow?
What do his coach and his friend think of Mimo?

«أيها السادة المشاهدون...
جائنا خَبرَ عاجِل. ميمو سُلطان، اللاعب المشهور في نادي المنصور اِختَفى تماماً قَبل كَأس العالَم غداً.»

«ميمو ولد مُتَهوِّر. غير معقول أن يكون هناك لاعب مُختفي من النادي قبل كأس العالم بِيَوم واحد ! غير مفهوم! غير مقبول!»

«ميمو أخي وصديقي، وهو مظلوم. ميمو لاعب كبير ومتمكّن لكن المدرّب ظَلَمَه.»

«يا ترى... هل يعود ميمو سلطان في الوقت المُناسب؟»

Match these Arabic words in the broadcast to their English meanings, as in the example.

| | |
|---|---|
| a) World Cup | ١ مُشاهِدون |
| b) capable | ٢ عاجِل |
| c) understandable | ٣ كَأس العالَم |
| d) disappearing | ٤ مُتهوِّر |
| e) wayward | ٥ مَعقول |
| f) reasonable | ٦ مُختَفي |
| g) viewers | ٧ مَفهوم |
| h) I wonder | ٨ مَظلوم |
| i) urgent | ٩ مُتَمَكِّن |
| j) wronged | ١٠ يا ترى |

## In summary

- Different nouns and adjectives can be formed from verbal roots.
- Nouns of place use the pattern مَفعل mafɛal.
- Verbal nouns vary for basic verbs but follow predictable patterns for the derived forms.
- Active and passive participles describe the doer and the receiver of an action.
- For basic verbs active participles are formed using the pattern فاعِل fāɛil and passive participles using the pattern مَفعول mafɛūl.
- Active participles and passive participles for the derived forms both begin with مُـ mu-. The active ends with kasra, e.g. مُستخدِم mustakhdim (user), and the passive with fatha: مُستخدَم mustakhdam (used).

unit 20

# Dual verbs

You have already seen in Unit 13 how Arabic has a dual ending ان -ān or ـَين -ayn which is added to nouns when referring to two of something. There are also special verb endings for 'they' and 'you' when the subject is dual.

ان -ān is added to the imperfect verbs:

*he travels* يُسافر yusāfir →
*they two travel* يُسافران yusāfirān

*you cooperate* yataعāwan يَتَعاوَن →
*you two cooperate* yataعāwanān يَتَعاوَنان

In the past, the dual ending is ا -ā:

*he attended* حَضَرَ ḥaḍara → *they two attended* حَضَرا ḥaḍarā

*you drank* شَرِبتَ sharibta → *you two drank* شَرِبتُما sharibtumā

The dual verb is relatively uncommon but you should at least be able to recognise it when you come across it. In English, it is often translated using the word 'both':

| | |
|---|---|
| *They both live in Cairo.* | هُما يَسكُنان في القاهِرة.<br>humā yaskunān fī l-qāhira. |
| *What did you both do yesterday?* | ماذا فعلتما أمس؟<br>mādhā faعaltumā ams? |

As with plural verbs (see Unit 14), if the verb comes *before* the dual subject, it will be in the *singular*:

> حَضَرَ الوزيران الاجتماع وتَعاوَنا في الخطّة.
> ḥaḍara al-wazīrān al-ijtimāع wa-taعāwanā fī l-khiṭṭa.
> *The two ministers attended the meeting and cooperated on the plan.*

## Activity 1

Rewrite these sentences in the dual, as in the example.

١ مَتَى تذهب إلى المدرسة؟ **مَتَى تذهبان إلى المدرسة؟**

٢ هل تَسكن في الكويت؟ ____________

٣ جلس الرَجُل وشرب فنجان قهوة. ____________

٤ هو مدرّس ويعمل في باريس. ____________

٥ إلى أين سافرتَ الصيف الماضي؟ ____________

٦ يُجَهِّز الطبّاخ الأكل ويُنَظِّف الأطباق. ____________

## In summary

- Arabic verbs have a dual form used with two subjects.
- In the imperfect tense, dual verbs end in ان-ān, e.g. يُسافران yusāfirān (they two travel), تُسافران tusāfirān (you two travel).
- In the past tense, dual verbs end in ا -ā , e.g. سافرا sāfarā (they two travelled), سافرتُما sāfartumā (you two travelled).

part 3

# Answers to activities

## UNIT 1

### *Activity 1*

1 ك/ت/ب k/t/b (core meaning: *writing*)
2 د/ر/س d/r/s (core meaning: *studying*)
3 ك/س/ر k/s/r (core meaning: *breaking*)
4 ل/ع/ب l/ع/b (core meaning: *playing*)

## UNIT 2

### *Activity 1*

1 مُذَكَّر (*masculine*) 2 مُؤَنَّث (*feminine*) 3 مُذَكَّر (*masculine*)
4 مُذَكَّر (*masculine*) 5 مُؤَنَّث (*feminine*) 6 مُذَكَّر (*masculine*)
7 مُذَكَّر (*masculine*) 8 مُؤَنَّث (*feminine*) 9 مُذَكَّر (*masculine*)
10 مُؤَنَّث (*feminine*) 11 مُؤَنَّث (*feminine*) 12 مُذَكَّر (*masculine*)

### *Optional Activity*

1 قميصٌ qamīṣ*un*
2 دجاجةٌ dajāja*tun*
3 بيتٌ bayt*un*
4 صورةٌ ṣūra*tun*
5 سيّارةٌ sayyāra*tun*
6 عينٌ ع‎ayn*un*

## UNIT 3

### *Activity 1*

1 المفتاح al-miftāḥ
2 الدجاجة ad-dajāja
3 القلم al-qalam
4 البيت al-bayt
5 الصورة aṣ-ṣūra
6 الممرّضة al-mumarriḍa
7 التين at-tīn
8 الخيمة al-khayma

### *Optional Activity*

1 المفتاحُ al-miftāḥ*u*
2 الدجاجةُ ad-dajāja*tu*
3 القلمُ al-qalam*u*
4 البيتُ al-bayt*u*
5 الصورةُ aṣ-ṣūra*tu*
6 الممرّضةُ al-mumarriḍa*tu*
7 التينُ at-tīn*u*
8 الخيمةُ al-khayma*tu*

# UNIT 4

### *Activity 1*

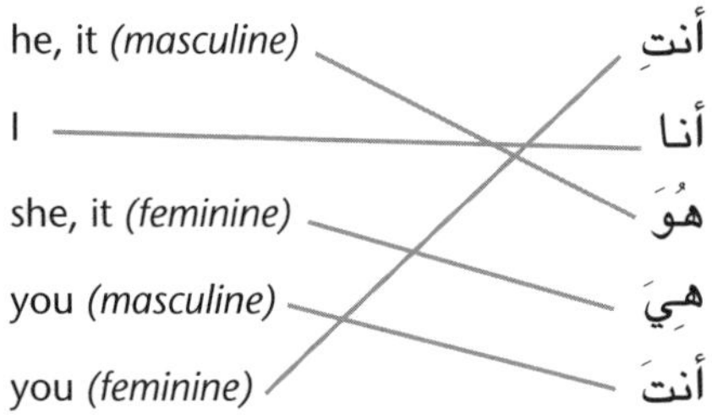


### *Activity 2*

1 أحمَد مدرّس.
2 أنا أنور.
3 أنتِ أُمّ سارة.
4 أنا في الحَديقة
5 هي ممرِّضة.

### *Activity 3*

1 هو مُدَرّس.
2 هي ممرّضة.
3 هو في الشارِع.
4 هي في الشارِع.
5 هو في الحديقة.
6 هي في السيّارة.

# UNIT 5

### *Activity 1*

1 هم مُهندِسون.
2 هم مِصريّون.
3 هم فَرَنسيّون.
4 هم خبّازون.
5 هم نجّارون.

### *Activity 2*

1 هُنَّ مُحاسبات.
2 نَحنُ عراقيّات.
3 هُنَّ فَرَنسيّات.
4 أنتُنَّ مصريات؟
5 لا، نَحنُ كُويتيّات.
6 هُنَّ مُهندِسات.

### *Activity 3*

1 هي مُحاسبة.
2 هم نجّارون
3 هنَّ مُمرّضات.
4 هو مُحاسب.
5 هو في الحقيبة.
6 هي في البيت.
7 هي في الشارع.

### *Optional Activity*

1 زجاجاتٌ zujājā*tun*
2 خبّازون khabbāzūn
3 حيواناتٌ ḥayawānā*tun*
4 لغاتٌ lughā*tun*
5 مهندسون muhandisūn
6 سيّاراتٌ sayyārā*tun*
7 مدرّساتٌ mudarrisā*tun*
8 اجتماعاتٌ ijtimāɛā*tun*

## UNIT 6

### *Activity 1*

1 هذا الرجل
2 هذه الحقيبة
3 تلك الجريدة
4 ذلك المدرّس
5 تلك الممرّضة
6 هذا القلم
7 هذا النهر
8 ذلك القميص

### *Activity 2*

1 هذه بنت.
2 هذا قلم.
3 هذا نهر.
4 هذه حقيبة.
5 تلك سيّارة.
6 هذا رجل.
7 ذلك رجل.
8 هذه ممرّضة.

### *Optional Activity*

1 هذا قلمٌ.
2 ذلك ولدٌ.
3 هذا الرجلُ خبّازٌ.
4 هذه مدرّسةٌ.
5 تلك الحقيبةُ كبيرةٌ.

### *Activity 3*

1 ✘ 2 ✔ 3 ✘ 4 ✔ 5 ✘ 6 ✘ 7 ✔ 8 ✔

## UNIT 7

### *Activity 1 (suggested answers)*

1 هذا البيت قديم.
2 هذه الحقيبة خفيفة.
3 هذا الولد قصير.
4 هذه البنت جميلة.
5 هذه الزجاجة مكسورة.
6 هذا الكلب مسرور.
7 هذه الخيمة كبيرة.
8 هذا النهر طويل.

### *Activity 2*

a) ٦ b) ٣ c) ٧ d) ٥ e) ١ f) ٢ g) ٤

### *Activity 3*

نـاديـة من بيروت. بيروت مدينـة كبيرة وجميلـة.
نـاديـة مُدرّسـة في مَدرسـة صغيرة. بيت نـاديـة قديم
وقريب من البَنك اللبنـاني والمَصنَع الجديد. نـاديـة
متزوّجـة وهـي مسرورة في عَمَلـها بـالمدرسـة.

### *Activity 4*

1 هذا الكتـاب أخضر.
2 هذه السيـّارة حمراء.
3 هذه الحقيبـة صفراء.
4 هذا القلم أزرق.
5 هذه الأقلام سوداء.
6 هذه الزجـاجـات خضـراء.
7 هذه السيـّارات صفراء وزرقـاء.
8 هذا الكلب أبيض وأسود.

### *Optional Activity*

١ هذا الرجلُ متزوّجٌ.
٢ البنتُ الصغيرةُ مسرورةٌ.
٣ النهرُ المشهورُ
٤ البيتُ الجديدُ قبيحٌ.
٥ هذه الجريدةُ قديمةٌ.
٦ سيّارةٌ كبيرةٌ.
٧ الحقيبـةُ خفيفـةٌ.

## UNIT 8

### *Activity 1*

*You should have drawn the following objects on the pictures:*

1. a bottle under the chair
2. a dog on the table
3. a pen in the bag
4. cars in front of the house
5. a bed next to the door on the right
6. a window between the cupboard and the chair

### *Activity 2*

1 البنك الجديد بجانب المدرسة .
2 فيصل مهندس في مصنع السيـّارات.
3 نـاديـة من بيروت في لبنـان.
4 هنـاك صورة صغيرة فوق الشبّـاك.

5 ذهبنا إلى مدينة قديمة.

6 هناك حقيبة ثقيلة على الكرسي.

***Activity 3***

هذا شارع كبير. في وَسَط الشارع هناك مَتحَف. هناك شجر طويل وراء المتحف وولد على درّاجة أمام المتحف. هناك مدرسة كبيرة بجانب المتحف.

على يمين المتحف هناك بيت قديم وجميل. الرجل مَعَ الكلب الأسود أمام البيت. وهناك طائِرة فوق البيت.

في الشارع هناك سيّارات وفي السيّارة البيضاء هناك إمرَأة وبنت.

***Optional Activity***

١ البنتُ في المدرسةِ. (The girl is in the school.)

٢ هناك قلمٌ على المائدةِ. (There's a pen on the table.)

٣ الولدُ بين الشبّاكِ والبابِ. (The boy is between the window and the door.)

٤ ذَهَبنا إلى المدينةِ. (We went to the town.)

٥ هناك نهرٌ جميلٌ في المدينةِ. (There's a beautiful river in the town.)

٦ هناك مصنعٌ جديدٌ بجانب النهرِ. (There's a new factory beside the river.)

# UNIT 9

***Activity 1***

1 نعم، هي تحت الكرسي.

2 لا، هم خَبّازون.

3 نعم، هي بيضاء.

4 نعم، هو كتاب.

5 لا، هو أمام الشجر.

6 لا، هو أسود.

***Activity 2***

١ أينَ ٢ ما ٣ ما ٤ كم ٥ بكم ٦ كيفَ ٧ متى ٨ لماذا

***Activity 3***

١ أنت من أين؟

٢ هو من أين؟

٣ كم زجاجةً على المائدة؟

٤ أين السيّارة؟

٥ متى الحفلة؟

٦ هل هناك بنك في المدينة؟

٧ ماذا كتب أحمد؟

### Optional Activity

١ كم بنتاً؟
٢ كم حقيبةً؟
٣ كم خيمةً؟
٤ كم قلماً؟
٥ كم كتاباً؟
٦ كم باباً؟

## UNIT 10

### Activity 1 (example sentences)

هذه درّاجة زينب.
هذه قطّة زينب.
هذه حقيبة زينب.
هذا كلب أحمد.
هذه سيّارة أحمد.
هذا قلم أحمد.
هذا كُمبيوترِ أحمد.

### Activity 2

1 سيّارة أحمد الجديد
2 قلم جيهان القديم
3 مهندسو المصنع
4 حقيبة الولد الثقيل
5 قميص محمّد الأبيض
6 خبّازو المدينة
7 شبّاك البيت الصغير
8 شركة المهندسين العراقيّين

### Activity 3

١ بيته baytuhu (baytuh)
٢ مدرستهم madrasatuhum (madrasathum)
٣ حالك ḥāluka (ḥālak)
٤ قلمها qalamuhā (qalamhā)
٥ سيّارتي sayyāratī
٦ مدينتنا madīnatunā (madīnatnā)
٧ كلبك kalbuki (kalbik)
٨ بيتكم baytukum (baytkum)

### Activity 4

١ أنا في بيتها.
٢ هل هذا كتابه؟
٣ لا، هذا كتابها.
٤ سيّاراتهم في الشارع.
٥ بابه أبيض.
٦ أين حقيبتهنّ؟
٧ مكتبهم الكبير قريب من المدرسة.
٨ كيف حالها؟

### Activity 5

a) ٦ b) ٤ c) ٧ d) ٢ e) ٣ f) ١ g) ٥

## UNIT 11

### *Activity 1*

١ بُنوك bunūk ٢ أولاد awlād ٣ فُعَل fuعal ٤ قُصور quṣūr ٥ أفعال afعāl

٦ جِبال jibāl ٧ فُعَل fuعal ٨ جَمَل jamal ٩ فِعال fiعāl ١٠ مَلِك malik

١١ فُعول fuعūl ١٢ أهرام ahrām ١٣ شَيخ shaykh ١٤ فُعول fuعūl

### *Activity 2*

١ g) ٢ c) ٣ d) ٤ h) ٥ j) ٦ b) ٧ i) ٨ e) ٩ a) ١٠ f)

### *Activity 3*

١ هذه القصور جميلة.
٢ السيّارات في الشَوارِع.
٣ اللُعَب بِجانِب الكُتُب .
٤ أين أقلامي الجديدة؟
٥ هناك جِبال طويلة.
٦ بُيوتنا بيضاء.
٧ المدرّسون مصريّون.
٨ الأهرام في الجيزة.
٩ الكُتُب القديمة على المَوائِد.
١٠ هذه صُوَر زينب.

### *Optional Activity*

١ هذه القصورُ جميلةٌ.
٢ السيّاراتُ في الشَوارِعِ.
٣ اللُعَبُ بِجانِبِ الكُتُبِ.
٤ أين أقلامي الجديدةُ؟
٥ هناك جِبالٌ طويلةٌ.
٦ بُيوتُنا بيضاءُ.
٧ المدرّسون مصريّون.
٨ الأهرامُ في الجيزةِ.
٩ الكُتُبُ القديمةُ على المَوائِدِ.
١٠ هذه صُوَرُ زينب.

## UNIT 12

### *Activity 1*

١ أقبَح ٢ أصغَر ٣ أقصَر ٤ أخَفّ ٥ أثقَل ٦ أقدَم ٧ أكثَر ٨ أسرَع

### *Activity 2*

١ بيتي أقدم من بيتك!
٢ أنا أغنى منك!
٣ مدينتي أجمل من مدينتك!
٤ حقيبتي أخفّ من حقيبتك!
٥ قميصي أجدّ من قميصك!
٦ أنا أسرع منك!
٧ سيّارتي أغلى من سيّارتك!
٨ خاتمي أكبر من خاتمك!

***Activity 3*** *(example sentences)*

كلب المدرّس أكبر من كلب المحاسب.
حقيبة المدرّس أثقل من حقيبة المحاسب.
قميص المدرّس أقدم من قميص المحاسب.
المحاسب أغنى من المدرّس.
بيت المحاسب أجمل من بيت المدرّس.
سيّارة المحاسب أجدّ وأسرع من سيّارة المدرّس .

***Activity 4***

١ أسرع ولد ٢ الأثقل ٣ أقدم بيت ٤ أكبر مدينة
٥ الأقصر ٦ أجدّ مهندس

## UNIT 13

***Activity 1***

١ عينان/عينَين ٢ كلبان/كلبَين ٣ درّاجتان/درّاجتَين
٤ مائدتان/مائدتَين ٥ بنتان/بنتَين ٦ سريران/سريرَين
٧ رجلان/رجلَين ٨ سيّارتان/سيّارتَين

***Activity 2***

a) ٣ b) ٦ c) ٥ d) ١ e) ٢ f) ٤

## UNIT 14

***Activity 1***

١ ذَهَبتُ ٢ جلَسَت ٣ وَجَدتَ ٤ شَرِبَ ٥ ذَهَبَت ٦ سَمِعتِ ٧ فَتَحتُ ٨ وَجَدَ

***Activity 2***

١ سارة مدرّسة. ذهبَت أمس إلى المدرسة...
٢ وفتحَت باب المدرسة.
٣ وجدَت سارة الكُتُب فوق المائدة.
٤ جلسَت على كرسي...
٥ وشربَت فِنجان شاى.
٦ ذهبَت الى الفَصل.
٧ بعد الدرس حضرَت اجتماع المدرّسين...
٨ ورَجَعَت الى بيتها.

### Activity 3

أنا مدرّسة. ذهبتُ أمس إلى المدرسة وفتحتُ باب المدرسة. وجدتُ الكُتُب فوق المائدة. جلستُ على كرسي وشربتُ فِنجان شاى. ذهبتُ الى الفَصل. بعد الدرس حضرتُ اجتماع المدرسين ورَجَعتُ الى بيتي.

### Activity 4

١ ذَهَبوا إلى المَصنع.
٢ خَرَجوا من البيت.
٣ جلَسنا في المكتب.
٤ هل سَمِعتُم الخبر؟
٥ حَضَرنَ الاجتماع.
٦ أين وَجَد المدرّسون مفتاح الباب؟
٧ ذَهَبنا الى بيت أُختنا.
٨ فتَحَ الأولاد الزُجاجة وشَرِبوا الكولا.

### Activity 5

١ ذَهَبتُ إلى البنك أمس.
٢ شَرِبَت فنجان قهوة.
٣ هل وَجَدتُم المِفتاح؟
٤ حَضَرنا الاجتِماع في المَصنَع.
٥ سَمِعَ أحمَد الخَبَر في المطعم.
٦ جلَسوا بِجانِب المدرّس.

### Optional Activity

١ فَتَحنا البابَ.
٢ وَجَدتُ الحَقيبةَ.
٣ وَجَدَ الولدُ كتاباً في الشارِعِ.
٤ هل سَمِعتَ الخبرَ في المَطعَمِ؟
٥ حَضَرَت المدرّسةُ اجتماعاً.
٦ شَرِبَ الرَجُلُ فنجانَ قهوةٍ.

## UNIT 15

### Activity 1

١ تغسِل وجهها صباحاً.
٢ يسكُن في الكُويت.
٣ تَشرَبينَ كولا؟
٤ أسكُن مَعَ أمّي.
٥ متّى تَخرُج من البيت؟
٦ تذهَب زينب إلى المكتب بالسيّارة.

### Activity 2

تسكُن نادية في القاهرة. كلّ يوم تَغسِل وجهها وتأكُل طَبَق فول. بَعدَ ذلك تَذهب إلى المدرسة بالأتوبيس وتَجلِس في الفَصل. تَرجع إلى البيت الساعة الثالثة. تَشرَب زجاجة كولا وتَلعَب مَعَ أصحابها في الحَديقة.

### Activity 3

١ يَغسِلونَ السيّارة يوم الجمعة.
٢ نسكن في بغداد.
٣ هل تَذهبون إلى البنك؟
٤ يَذهب الأولاد إلى الحديقة ويلعبون تَنِس.
٥ الكلاب تفتح الباب.
٦ نرجَع من المكتَب ونشرب فنجان شاي.

### *Activity 4*

١ هو مدرّس ويعمل في مدرسة.
٢ هي مدرّسة وتعمل في مدرسة.
٣ هو محاسب ويعمل في بنك.
٤ هم مهندسون ويعملون في مصنع.
٥ هو طبّاخ ويعمل في مطعم.
٦ هم خبّازون ويعملون في مخبز.
٧ هنّ ممرّضات ويعملنَ في مستشفى.

### *Activity 5*

١ وَجَدناها تحت الكرسي.
٢ هل وجدتَه؟
٣ سوف أشربه.
٤ غسلَتها فاطمة.
٥ سمعتُه في الراديو.
٦ كلّ يوم يَحضُرونَه.
٧ سمعِناهم في الشارع.
٨ سنفتحه بَعدَ ساعة.

## UNIT 16

### *Activity 1*

١ كُلّ يوم نَجِد قطّة في الشارع.
٢ كُلّ يوم أصِل إلى المَكتب صباحاً.
٣ كُلّ يوم تصِف نادية رِحلتها إلى باريس.
٤ كُلّ يوم يجِدون المِفتاح على المائدة.
٥ كُلّ يوم يزِن الخبّاز العَجين.
٦ كُلّ يوم يصِل إلى وسط المدينة بالقِطار.

### *Activity 2*

١ عُدتُ ٢ سنَزور ٣ بِعتِ ٤ يَبيعونَ ٥ قالَت ٦ باعَ ٧ تَطير ٨ فازَت

### *Activity 3*

| Past | Future |
|---|---|
| ١ كنتُ في المَصنَع. | ١ سأكون في المَصنَع. |
| ٢ كُنّا في المدرسة. | ٢ سَنكون في المدرسة. |
| ٣ كانَت أختي مُقيمة في السَعودية. | ٣ سَتكون أختي مُقيمة في السَعودية. |
| ٤ كانوا في المدرسة. | ٤ سَيكونون في المدرسة. |
| ٥ هل كُنتِ في بيتك؟ | ٥ هل سَتكونين في بيتك؟ |

### Activity 4

1 He wanted to travel to London (لندن); 2 He wanted to visit his brother, Shalabi; 3 He had to go to the airline company office (مكتب شركة الطيران) in the centre of town (وسط المدينة); 4 He had to wait three days (ثلاثة أيّام); 5 The children find waiting three days for a ticket funny as they're used to instant internet purchases.

قال الحاجّ خيري لأحفاده...
«شبكة الانترنت هي سوق لِمَن يشتري أو يبيع أيّ شيء وكُلّ شيء. مُنذُ سَنَوات، ذَهَبتُ لِشِراء تذكِرة أطير بها إلى لندَن لأزور أخي شلبي المُقيم هناك. كان مكتب شَرِكة الطَيران بعيداً في وسط المدينة. دَفعنا ثمَن التذكرة ثم قالوا لنا: حِين تعودون بعد ثلاثة أيّام سَتكون التذكرة مَوجودة.»
ضَحِكَ الأولاد وهم يقولون «ها! ها! ثلاثة أيام لشراء تذكرة!»

### Activity 5

رَدَدتُ أشُكّ تَدُلّينَ نَظُنّ عَدَدتُ مدَّت ضَمّوا

### Activity 6

١ مدَّت ٢ رَدَدتُ ٣ عَدَدتُ ٤ أشُكّ ٥ نَظُنّ ٦ ضَمّوا

### Activity 7

1 ✔ 2 ✘ 3 ✘ 4 ✘ 5 ✔ 6 ✔ 7 ✘ 8 ✔ 9 ✘ 10 ✔

أنا مُدَرِّب التَنِس في النادي، وأنا من بيروت في لُبنان. في الماضي كُنتُ مهندساً في مصنع ولكنّي الآن أرى أن حياة المدرّب أفضَل.
صباح كلّ يوم، أشرَب فنجان شاي، وآكُل سَندَويتش جُبنة ثم آخذ الباص إلى نادي التنس.
أَصِف للأولاد والبنات كيف يمسكون المضارب ويردّون الكرة فوق الشبكة، وأقول «عينك على الكرة دائماً!».
في المساء أعود إلى بيتي وأحياناً أزور أختي أو ألعب الشَطرَنج مع أصحابي.

## UNIT 17

### Activity 1

*Form II; Form IV; Form III; Form II; Form III; Form IV; Form II; Form III; Form II*

### Activity 2

a) ٣ b) ٦ c) ٢ d) ٥ e) ١ f) ٤

### Activity 3

١ هل صَوّرتَ الحَيَوانات؟
٢ سافَروا إلى فَرَنسا بالطائرة.
٣ دَرّبَ بشير الأولاد في النادي.
٤ أحَضَرَت الممَرّضة الدواء.
٥ عامَلتُ الضُيوف كَأصحابي.
٦ أكَلنا الطُيور.

### Activity 4

السَيِّد جونز من ويلز ويُحاول أن يَتَعَلَّم العَرَبية. مُستَواه يَتَقَدَّم مع كلّ دَرس لأنّه يحاول أن يتذكّر الكَلمات العَرَبية. حين يَتَقابَل الناس في الشارع صباحاً، يَتَبادَلون التَحيّة والسلام ويقولون: «صباح الخير!» سَألَ السَيِّد جونز المدرّس عن الرَدّ المُناسِب، وتَدَرَّبَ على قول «صباح النور!» لِمُدة يَومَين.

| | | |
|---|---|---|
| practise تَدَرَّب/يَتَدَرَّب | meet up تَقابَل/يَتَقابَل | learn تَعَلَّم/يَتَعَلَّم |
| exchange تَبادَل/يَتَبادَل | progress تَقَدَّم/يَتَقَدَّم | remember تَذَكَّر/يَتَذَكَّر |

### Activity 5

١ تُحاول أن تتعلّم العربيّة.
٢ تذكّرتُ الكلمات العربيّة.
٣ حين نتقابل، نتبادلون التحيّة.
٤ تقولين: «صباح الخير.»
٥ سألوا عن الردّ المناسب.
٦ تدرّبتَ على قول «صباح النور».

### Activity 6

| Form | Present/future | Past | Meaning |
|---|---|---|---|
| *VIII* | yaqtarib يَقتَرِب | iqtaraba اِقتَرَب | *to approach* |
| *X* | yastamtiع يَستَمتِع | istamtaعa اِستَمتَع | *to enjoy* |
| *VII* | yanqalib يَنقَلِب | inqalaba اِنقَلَبَ | *to be overturned* |
| *VIII* | yastamiع يَستَمِع | istamaعa اِستَمَعَ | *to listen* |
| *X* | yastaḥsin يَستَحسِن | istaḥsana اِستَحسَن | *to admire* |
| *VIII* | yabtakir يَبتَكِر | ibtakara اِبتَكَرَ | *to create* |
| *X* | yastakhdim يَستَخدِم | istakhdama اِستَخدَمَ | *to use* |

*Activity 7*

١ هل تستخدم شَبكة الانترنت في مكتبك؟ ٢ يستخدمون شَبكة الانترنت في مكتبهم. ٣ اقترب الباص من الشارع الرئيسي. ٤ اقترنا من بيتنا. ٥ أستمع إلى الأخبار في الراديو. ٦ هل استمتعتُم بالفيلم؟

## UNIT 18

*Activity 1*

١ لا تأخُذ فاطمة الأوتوبيس إلى المدرسة. ٢ لا يغسل أحمد وجهه صباحاً. ٣ لا أتحدّث العَرَبيّة. ٤ لا تُسخِّنينَ الخبز في الفرن. ٥ لا يَجلس الأولاد في الفَصل ولا يَدرسونَ اللغة العربيّة. ٦ لا نَسكُن في وَسَط المدينة.

*Activity 2*

١ لا أشرب كولا. ٢ لا نسافر بالطائرة. ٣ لا تدرس العربيّة. ٤ لا يستمتع بالكُتُب. ٥ لا يبيعون الدرّاجات.

*Activity 3*

١ ذَهَبتُ/أُقابِل ٢ ذَهَبَت/تَجِد ٣ تكتُب ٤ سافَرنا/نَستَمتِع ٥ اشتَرى/يَستَخدِم ٦ يَستَمِعوا/كَسَروا

*Activity 4*

1 ✗ 2 ✓ 3 ✓ 4 ✗ 5 ✓ 6 ✗ 7 ✗

*Activity 5*

أُحب أن أُسافر بالطائرة ولكنّي لا أُحب البَحر. في الصيف الماضي لم آخذ الطائرة وسافرتُ بالمركب في رِحلة تستَغرِق يَومين. كانت رِحلة عَذاب لأنّي لم أُجهِّز نَفسي للسَفَر بالمركب أَبَداً...
لم أَحجِز قمَرَة خاصّة. لم أَستمع إلى النشرة الجويّة في الراديو.
لم أُحضِر حُبوب دوار البحر. ولم أَلبس قُبَعتي في الشمس.
قُلتُ لِطَبيب المركب «أنا لا أستمتع بالمَراكِب يا دكتور. أنا لا أُريد أن أرى حتى صورة مَركِب في حَياتي بعد اليوم.»

## UNIT 19

*Activity 1*

١ مَجالِس ٢ مَداخِل ٣ مَكاتِب ٤ مَخارِج ٥ مَعارِض ٦ مَتاحِف ٧ مَلاعِب ٨ مَسارِح

### *Activity 2*

١ نريد زِيارة المتحف.
٢ نريد الذَهاب إلى البنك.
٣ أريد كِتابة رِسالة لأمّي.
٤ أحبّ الخروج من البيت.
٥ تُحبّ نادية اللَعِب مع أصحابها.
٦ يَجِب علينا العَودة إلى المكتب.

### *Activity 3*

'My life is a struggle. My husband is a journalist in the Ministry of Information and his mission in life is the fight against hypocrisy and corruption.

Our one disagreement is that he doesn't find the time to help me in preparing the food, or teaching anything to the children, or in mending this or cleaning that. Just as remembering occasions, talking to the family and sending flowers are all only my responsibility.'

«حياتي كِفاح. زوجي صَحَفي في وِزارة الإعلام ورِسالته في الحياة هي النِضال ضد النِفاق والفَساد.

خِلافنا الوحيد هو أنّه لا يجد الوَقت ليُساعِدني في تَجهيز الأكل، أو تدريس شَيء للأولاد، أو في تصليح هذا أو تنظيف تلك. كما أن تذكُّر المُناسبات، ومُحادثة الأُسرة، وإرسال الزُهور كلّها مَسئوليّتي أنا وَحدي.»

### *Activity 4*

١ الاستماع ٢ الانقلاب ٣ الاجتماع ٤ استقبال ٥ اقتراب/الامتحان

### *Activity 5*

It's the World Cup tomorrow. Mimo's coach thinks he's wayward and his behaviour irresponsible, but his friend thinks it's the coach's fault.

a) ٣ b) ٩ c) ٧ d) ٦ e) ٤ f) ٥ g) ١ h) ١٠ i) ٢ j) ٨

## UNIT 20

### *Activity 1*

١ مَتَى تذهبان إلى المدرسة؟
٢ هل تسكنان في الكويت؟
٣ جلس الرجلان وشربا فنجان قهوة.
٤ هما مدرّسان ويعملان في باريس.
٥ إلى أين سافرتُما الصيف الماضي؟
٦ يُجَهِّز الطبّاخان الأكل وينظّفان الأطباق.